SGT. DINWIDDIE'S WAR

SGT. DINWIDDIE'S WAR

B-17s, POWs AND THE BELGIAN UNDERGROUND IN WORLD WAR II

BY

TERRY H. IRWIN

Acclaim Press
MORLEY, MISSOURI

Acclaim Press
— Your Next Great Book —
P.O. Box 238
Morley, MO 63767
(573) 472-9800
www.acclaimpress.com

Book & Cover Design: Frene Melton

ISBN: 978-1-956027-14-3 | 1-956027-14-9
Library of Congress Control Number: 2021949385

First Printing: 2022
Printed in the United States of America
10 9 8 7 6 5 4 3 2 1

CONTENTS

DEDICATION

This work is dedicated to the young men of the Fowler crew: Don, Jim, Barney, Joe, Al, Curt, Richard, Loren, Jack, Miller, and Harry. May their courage, dedication to duty, and memories live on. *We must never forget them.*

To my good friend Steven Ruffin, Colonel, USAF. Without his guidance (since the 6th grade, actually) this book would have never come to fruition.

Most importantly, I would like to extend my loving gratitude to my wife, Donna, for first suggesting that I write this for the grandkids. This is especially dedicated to her for the encouragement and support that she gave during the project. It couldn't have happened without her help.

ACKNOWLEDGMENTS

I want to give my appreciation to Jean Amick Dinwiddie and Kim Dinwiddie Gillam for their contributions. Jean graciously shared her collection of documents and photos of her husband's war years, and Kim told me of the recollections of things her father shared about the war as she was growing up.

The conversations and emails that I shared with Barney Rawlings years ago were immensely important, giving me a view from the copilot's seat in the *G.I. Sheets* on that last mission.

A huge thank you goes out to French historian Greg Celerse for sharing with me the valuable information he discovered that helped tell the real story of what happened to Don and Jim Fowler in Lille, France, in May 1944.

SGT. DINWIDDIE'S WAR

B-17s, POWs and the Belgian Underground in World War II

chapter one

MISSION ON!

It was a cold Saturday morning, January 29, 1944. The wake-up call came at 0400, and it wasn't gentle. There was a fist banging on the door, then the shadowy figure of the orderly was behind the flashlight shining on your face. The booming "Mission on, roll out!" was the introduction to the coming hard day in the life of a bomber crewman.

The crews were seldom given official advanced notice of when a mission was going to occur. There were German spies and sympathizers everywhere, even in England, and the longer a mission could be kept quiet, the better the chance of surprising the enemy. You'd go to bed at night not knowing what tomorrow held, but there were subtle indicators of a mission being in the works. Things like the maintenance crews testing engines and pumping fuel, or the lights being on late in the weather office and the operations shack. Another sign was more activity in the mess halls, with the cooks and their helpers fussing with supplies for an early breakfast. A not-so-subtle sign was the sound of the strings of bomb carts being pulled by tractors, rattling and clanking like freight trains of destruction, hauling bombs to the B-17s parked on the hardstands. The experienced crews of the 303rd Bomb Group had come to learn the familiar signs, and they'd try to get the needed rest, but sleep was hard to come by when you thought too much about the mission and what it entailed.

The crews would hit the mess halls in thirty minutes. If you were on a crew, you would be getting out of bed into the cold room you shared with three other men, then you headed to the lavatory for a quick splash of cold water on your face and grab your razor for a close shave. Most of the flight would be over 10,000 feet on a mission, so you'd have to use your oxygen mask, and you didn't want it to chafe your face. More importantly, it needed to seal well, or you might not have a good flow of oxygen. Although everyone tried to keep an eye on their fellow crew members, men had passed out and had even died from the lack of oxygen. You couldn't stop the fear in your gut, or the cold at high altitude, or the accuracy of the Kraut gunners or fighter pilots, but you could make the effort to make sure you kept breathing, and it was something to do to keep from dwelling on that stuff you couldn't do anything about during the next several hours. So, you shaved and got your gear together, then you went to the chow hall.

The crews of the 303rd at RAF Molesworth were like the others assigned all over East Anglia. The B-17 and the B-24 were the heavy bombers used by the 8th Air Force, and both were usually flown by a crew of ten men. The 303rd flew the B-17 out of Molesworth, which was officially still owned by the Royal Air Force but had been turned over to the U.S. Army Air Force for the duration of the war. The RAF had flown lighter aircraft out of the field, and before the Americans could use it, the runways had to be strengthened and made longer. More buildings were constructed for maintenance, administration and for housing the personnel. The field was still called RAF Molesworth, and there might be an occasional British military person seen there, but it was generally a USAAF field, one of over a hundred similar fields scattered over the English countryside.

The Americans started making their presence known shortly after coming into the European war after December 7, 1941. The Japanese bombed the U.S. Navy Pacific Fleet at Pearl Harbor on that date, and a few days later Hitler declared war on the United States. The current war had started in Europe on September 1, 1939, when Hitler's troops marched into Poland. By the time the United States entered the war in late 1941, the Nazi armies had rolled swiftly over just about all of Europe. All of Continental Europe with the major exceptions of Switzerland, Spain and Portugal were under German rule. Hitler's troops stopped on the French shores of the English Channel, massed for an invasion of England that never occurred. But the Luftwaffe relentlessly bombed major cities in Great Britain from the time period roughly from October 1940 through July 1941. While historians disagree on the dates of what has been called "The Battle of Britain", the time period mentioned above takes into consideration two major German bombing campaigns aimed at trying to get Great Britain to negotiate a surrender. The British never backed down, and the Germans never invaded. By the time the United States entered the war, Germany had all but given up on England, but Hitler's army and air force occupied almost all of Europe. Furthermore, the German navy owned the Atlantic Ocean, and U-boats were seemingly everywhere. When the United States entered the war, a new strategic plan was being put into place, and it was something that had never been seen before in the history of warfare. It was a great experiment, and nobody knew if it would be successful. But the fate of the world depended on it.

The experiment came out of necessity. From mid-1940 until the time the U.S. bombers came to England in 1942, Hitler had control of all of Western Europe. There were no land-based Allied troops to oppose the German forces. The British had troops in France but had to engage in a humiliating retreat, pulling out at Dunkirk under the threat of losing all their forces to the Germans. As it was, between May 26, 1940 and June 4, 1940, 330,000 Allied troops (British and French) retreated across the Channel to safety, but the British lost approximately 66,000 men in the failed challenge to the German forces.

After Dunkirk, there were no Allied ground troops in Europe, and the only war that could be fought was from the air. It is important to know that until the United States sent heavy bombers to be based in the United Kingdom in 1942, the British were fighting an air war that was primarily carried out at night. The British bombers left their bases in England near dusk or later, fly to targeted cities in occupied Europe, and attempted to bomb those cities in hopes of destroying German facilities and personnel. It was literally a hit-or-miss proposition, because bombing at night was not accurate nor very effective. The British didn't label it so, but it was basically terror bombing, hoping that the strikes in the night would demoralize the German troops and citizens, hopefully making them lose the desire to engage in the war. Demoralizing as it might be to the enemy, the British bombing campaign was doing little to slow any German expansion of the war. Something else needed to be done.

The United States had been working to make aerial bombing more accurate and predictable. If bombs could be put on specific targets with consistent accuracy, then it would be possible to destroy strategic elements of the enemy infrastructure and military forces. For example, if you knew where a railway yard was located that was a major transportation hub of the Germans, destroying it would slow or stop supplies and troops from being moved efficiently. Destroying oil refineries would deny the enemy fuel for his aircraft and vehicles. The Americans had faith that this plan would work, because they possessed an invention that could promise consistent accuracy in dropping bombs on particular targets.

The instrument that the Americans possessed was the Norden bombsight. It was developed by Carl Norden, a Dutch engineer who had been educated in Switzerland and had moved to the United States in the early 1900s.

He had figured out a way to plot the course of a bomb dropped by an aircraft in order to predict its path to a target, then he built a mechanical aiming device that could be carried in the aircraft to perform this task. He started working on the device in the early 1920s, but it wasn't perfected into a useful piece of bombing equipment until 1939. The Norden bombsight was a closely guarded secret before and in the first years of the war, second only to the secret development of the atomic bomb.

With the Norden bombsight and the development of the B-17 and B-24 four-engine bombers, it was thought that the American air force could hit particular strategic targets to cripple the German war effort, but to hit those targets from high altitude, the attack had to be made in daylight with clear weather. The British thought that such a plan was suicidal, and that the possible results would be too costly in losses of aircraft and crews. After all, with every bomber shot down, ten men could potentially be lost to being killed or taken prisoner. The Americans were gambling with the lives of their airmen, but as stated earlier, it was a risk they were willing to take. In 1942, the only plan on the table to defeat the Germans was to take the war to the enemy in the air, to bomb his cities, refineries, transportation hubs, ship yards, troop concentrations, and factories. If the British bombed at night, and the Americans bombed during the day, perhaps the constant barrage of bombs would soften up the enemy and make a land-based invasion a viable possibility at a later date. The only problem with this plan is that it had never been done before. The science of bombing the enemy into submission would have to be perfected as it was being carried out. Still, it was the only game in town. Trying to fight the Germans on the ground in Continental Europe had been found to be an unworkable proposition. The British had learned that painful realization at Dunkirk. If the Germans could be attacked and broken by aerial bombardment first, then a ground invasion (if carried out at the proper time and place) might work.

The Americans were coming over in huge numbers to put their audacious plan into action. First, airfields had to be constructed or modified. Crews had to be trained. Aircraft had to be built and delivered to the new airfields. It was an endeavor on a scale never to have been seen before or since. The 8th Air Force was created and, led by General Ira Eaker, was sent to England. All of the airmen, fighter planes, and bombers were part of the "Mighty Eighth". How successful it would be was yet to be seen.

By the time of today's mission in late January 1944, the Americans had been dropping bombs on German-occupied territory for a little over a year. The jury was still out as to whether this plan was working as well as they had hoped. Some of the missions seemed to be as the British had predicted…suicidal. The losses sometimes were high, and the targets weren't destroyed. Sometimes the missions were "milk runs", with little trouble, but the targets weren't destroyed then, either. All kinds of factors went into whether or not a mission was effective. The weather was always a problem, but there were advances being made on how to bomb through the clouds using radio for navigation. That was still in the early stages and wasn't too useful. Like the weather, another factor always present were the German defenses. Anti-aircraft guns of the enemy were seeming to get better with each mission. So were the fighters. German fighter planes like the Messerschmitt Me-109 and the twin-engine Me-110 were feared by the bomber crews. The Focke Wulf 190 was devastatingly effective. All of these fighters were fitted with 20mm cannons, machine guns that fired slower, but fired larger projectiles. And to make it worse, some of the 20mm bullets were fitted with charges that exploded on impact. All of these things put fear into the American bomber crews, and that in itself was a problem. A man could only take so much stress and fear before he couldn't do his job. Again, bombing on this scale had never been done before, so the 8th Air Force was making the rules and standards as the war was being fought.

There was an arbitrary number that had been established by the 8th Air Force to mark the end of a crewman's tour of duty. If he made it through twenty-five missions, then he was due for rotation back to the states or into another non-combat job in England. Any crewman who made it to the vaunted twenty-fifth mission was heaped with praise and accolades. The only problem was that a crewman had a one in ten chance of making it through twelve missions if you looked at the statistics. Everyone hoped they'd be one of the fortunate ones…like Captain Edward "Woody" Woddrup, a pilot in the 427th Squadron. Woddrup had volunteered with the British Royal Air Force before the United States was in the war and had survived several night bombing missions as a pilot. Then, when the United States came into the war, he switched over to U.S. Army Air Force as a B-17 pilot and flew his twenty-five missions, then stayed on for another six. He had his scrapes and incidents but made it through it alive. It was interesting that Woody could have probably avoided the war entirely, because he came from a prominent family with a lot of political influence. He was one of the heirs to the Singer Sewing Machine Company. But he willingly chose to fight.

Another crew to emulate was that of Captain Billy Southworth. He and his crew made it to twenty-five missions with no sweat. Southworth was a professional baseball player but joined the air force to fight the Germans. His father was the manager of the St. Louis Cardinals, and when Billy flew his missions, he always wore a Cardinal ball cap instead of his air force cap. Non-regulation apparel was against the rules, but he always said that his baseball cap made his headphones fit better. Nobody seemed to mind…he got the job done.

But for every Woddrup or Southworth crew, there were many more who didn't make it to twenty-five missions. And there were those who came back from a mission in a shot-up aircraft with wounded or dead crew members on board. Sometimes a plane would make it through a mission unscathed, but with a crew member dead from oxygen starvation because of an oxygen system malfunction, or a gunner with frostbite so bad that he had to be hospitalized.

And that twenty-five mission goal? It was later increased to thirty missions, because the leaders of the 8th Air Force decided that it was better to keep experienced crews on the job longer, and not to rotate them out after twenty-five missions. To most of the bomber crews, it was almost as if the generals were *trying* to kill them.

One of the most problematic situations facing the daylight bombing campaign in 1942 was the fact that the bombers had to fly deeper and deeper into the German-occupied territories in order to strike the necessary targets. To do so was to put the bombers at a higher risk because of the lack of fighters to escort them to and from the targets. German fighters were based throughout France, Belgium, and the Netherlands, and they didn't have to fly far in order to attack the bombers. On the other hand, Allied fighter escorts had limited range, and could not fly with the bombers all the way to the target. After the development of the drop tank, fighters could carry more fuel and could escort the bombers further into their missions, thus reducing bomber losses.

The "learn-as-you-go" method of developing an effective bombing campaign produced many problems that had to be solved. A seemingly simple problem was how to lubricate the machine guns on the bombers. The B-17 was named the "Flying Fortress" because it was defended by ten to thirteen machine guns, the number depending on the model of the aircraft.

The Browning Model M-2 .50 caliber machine gun was a fearsome weapon, capable of firing 750 rounds per minute (twelve per second), with each bullet having an effective range of over 1/2 mile. The problem with guns of this type is that they had to be effectively lubricated in order to work properly. On the ground, even on a winter day, this wasn't a problem. However, a typical bomber mission was flown at an altitude of 18,000 to 26,000 feet, where the air temperature would be as much as -50 degrees Fahrenheit, and normal lubricants would thicken and not be effective. Gunners had to contend with frozen and jammed guns and trying to fix them during a fighter attack was nearly impossible. Necessity being the mother of invention, in time effective gun grease was finally developed.

Another serious problem was how to keep the gunners protected from frostbite. The waist gunners, firing out of open ports on each side of the rear portion of the fuselage, were faced with a brutally frigid wind blowing past during the entire mission. Heavy clothing impeded their movement, and one of the developments to give warmth and freedom of movement was the electrically heated flying suit. The suit's fabric was embedded with heated wires, similar to the construction of an electric blanket. Plugged into the aircraft's electrical system, it was theoretically possible to keep the airmen warm at high altitude. Once again, the theory was good, but the first suits proved to present problems of shorting out and catching fire. Until they were perfected, early crew members found themselves having to undress in the freezing plane to escape a smoldering suit. Added to that, the suits were constructed of a fuzzy light blue material that made them resemble a child's pajamas, and the early examples were nicknamed "bunny suits".

Again and again there were other ideas that had to be perfected, equipment invented and modified, new materials developed in order to allow the bombing to continue successfully. By the mission on January 29, 1944, the learning curve had leveled, and the missions were being flown with more routine and fewer problems. That didn't apply to the fear level, however. Fear was always a problem.

After splashing cold water on your face and shaving, getting dressed was the next ritual. The flying gear was more or less standard for everyone. The pilot, copilot, navigator, bombardier and radioman had heated compartments, but the gunners had to dress for the cold. For every thousand feet of altitude, the temperature dropped roughly 3 degrees.

At a typical mission altitude of 25,000 feet, the temperature would be 75 degrees colder than that on the ground at Molesworth. Heated compartments or not, *all* the crewmen had to also dress for the unthinkable. Nobody wanted to admit that they might have to bail out, but part of the equipment necessary was the issued survival kit. It included some candy and chocolate, French money, a small map and compass, and a small language card with necessary words translated to French and Dutch stating that you were an American airman. Some crewmen added to the kit things that they thought they might need, like hunting knives, or the old Colt .45 revolver that Grandpa had given you before you shipped out. Personal weapons were actually prohibited, but there seemed to be little interest in enforcing that rule.

Technically, everything you needed was supplied, and all you were permitted to take on a mission was the provided equipment. Personal items like wallets, letters from home, etc, were not allowed. All you were supposed to have that could identify you were your dog tags. Everything else was left behind, hopefully waiting for your safe return. But what if you didn't make it back?

Some crewmen had their personal belongings packed and ready to be sent home in the event they didn't return. Others left their personal effects just like they were, refusing to acknowledge that there was a chance that they wouldn't return safely, and that packing the stuff would hasten your demise in the coming mission.

Superstition played a large role in the minds of some airmen, and in spite of the regulations, it was a rare crewman that didn't tuck some lucky talisman into his flight gear. A picture of a wife or girlfriend, an old pocket watch your grandfather gave you, a rabbit's foot, etc, was more often than not hidden in a pocket for the ride to the target and back. One pilot once took a stuffed teddy bear that had belonged to his child. The mission was successful and had no problems, and because of that, the whole crew adopted the lucky teddy bear and made sure it was sitting on the instrument panel on every mission. And, yes, pilot and bear made through the war safely.

After getting dressed and ready to go, the crews wandered to the mess hall. Usually eggs for breakfast are a good thing for most people. But eggs to some bomber crews took on a superstitious role, an indicator of how bad the mission would be. If the mission was predicted to be rough, it was thought that the orders had gone to the mess hall staff to "feed the boys well, they're going to need it on this one today". That was a common thought, whether factual or not.

On this morning, they got real eggs, not the powdered ones of a non-mission breakfast, and you could have two or three of them if you wanted and thought you could hold them down. Yeah, the mission today looked like it could be a rough one according to the egg availability. But then, they were all rough, some just rougher than others. Any mission you were about to fly was bad, the fear compounding the evils waiting for you in the enemy's airspace.

The crews had an hour for breakfast. Most of the enlisted crews sat together in their area, and the officers sat together in their appointed area. After eating, they had time to meet with a chaplain for a quick service if they wished, time to go to the bathroom to relieve themselves (the first of many times before takeoff), and then head to the mission briefing.

An interesting note about chaplains. Molesworth, like most of the small fields, didn't have a chaplain for every faith, but they had chaplains for any faith. It was common for a service to include various faiths all served by whatever chaplain was available. For a pre-mission service, most of the men weren't too picky about who prayed for them but were pleased to know that an extra voice speaking in God's ear couldn't hurt their situation.

An important part of the mission, other than flying it, was the briefing. All of the crewmen attended the general briefing; afterwards, there were separate briefings for pilots, navigators, bombardiers, and gunners. At the general briefing the target would be revealed, the routes to and from the target would be gone over, and the weather and an estimate of enemy defenses would be discussed. But it was always the location of the target that was on everyone's mind. Some targets were considered milk runs; others were meat grinders. Today's mission was a meat grinder. When the curtain in front of the mission map was pulled open, there were groans when the crews saw the red string stretching from RAF Molesworth to Frankfurt, Germany. Located in the industrial area of the Ruhr Valley, it was heavily defended. The Ruhr had been attacked many times and had been given the moniker "Happy Valley", because the flak, fighters, and weather made it anything *but* happy. Maybe the breakfast superstition was right…this was definitely shaping up to be a three-egg mission. It was also announced that this was to be the largest bombing mission of the war, a joint mission involving almost 1,000 bombers (B-17s and B-24s) from several bases in England, plus hundreds of British and American escort fighters.

After the crews left the general briefing, they headed to their individual meetings, which were relatively short. After that, they went to their assigned aircraft. Contrary to what movies and television would have us believe, crews were usually assigned to a different aircraft on each mission and didn't have one plane that was "theirs". They might have contributed to the naming of it, and maybe even had nose art painted on it, and maybe had a favorite plane or one they didn't like, but the planes were rotated between crews, with some planes staying in maintenance while others flew. The mission today was to be a "maximum effort", which meant that all available planes would be on the mission, and some in the air as spares if needed to replace the assigned aircraft that might develop mechanical problems. The spares would return to Molesworth if not needed. Thirty-nine B-17s from the 303rd would be in the air, coming from the four squadrons that made up the group: the 358th, 359th, 360th, and 427th.

One important item in the briefing was the bomb loading. A normal load for the early B-17s was 4,000 lbs., but with improved engines, the bomb load had evolved upward to 6,000 lbs. in the latest models of the aircraft. The weather conditions also dictated how much the bomber could carry—cooler temperatures allowed the load to be heavier. The load for today's mission to Frankfurt was 6,000 lbs. for most aircraft. That consisted of twelve 500 lb. bombs. The bombardiers were released from their briefing to be at the aircraft first. After getting target information and photos at the briefing, the next job, a very important one, was to check the bomb loading and fusing. The bombs had been loaded the night before as the crews were trying to sleep, but the installation of the fuses was done just before takeoff. In the earlier days of the bombing campaign, the fuses were installed in the air, en route to the target. Several accidents had occurred during the airborne fusing, so that plan was abandoned in favor of fusing the bombs just before taking off. It was not a common occurrence, but there had been accidents with that procedure, also. Of course, an aircraft that had an accident on takeoff could create a disastrous explosion, but there had also been accidents during the fusing process. One moment an aircraft was sitting on the hardstand, and instantly there would be a huge flash and a rush of thunderous noise, and the aircraft and anyone near it just ceased to exist.

Nobody wanted to be near a loaded bomber during fusing unless they were required to be there, and not even then was anyone ever comfortable with the situation. The bombers of the 303rd Bomb Group, like on all bomber fields, were parked around the outskirts of the installation on hardstands, separated from one another to prevent an accident with one plane from spreading to the others.

The bombardier on every crew also had another task that he was charged with doing...installing the super-secret Norden bombsight. The sights were so secret that they were kept in special vaults with guards watching over them. When the mission was about to go, the bombardier would take his sight to the aircraft that was assigned to him for installation. After putting it in place, certain mechanisms had to be aligned and set to insure its accuracy. Once the sight was taken out of the vault, it was the bombardier's to guard with his life. If the aircraft was hit by enemy fire and the crew had to abandon ship, or if the plane made a forced landing in enemy territory, he was ordered to destroy the sight to keep it out of enemy hands. Ironically, by the time of this mission, both the Germans and Japanese had salvaged Norden bombsights from crashed planes and had figured out how it operated, so the secrecy was unnecessary. In addition, neither the Germans nor Japanese had need for such a device, because at this point in the war, both countries were starting to fight a defensive war and had no means of performing bombing missions like those in which the Americans were engaged.

At any rate, the bombardiers had made it to their assigned planes, fused the bombs, installed and set up the secret bombsights, and sat in the plexiglass nose compartments and looked over the target photos, Colt .45 pistols by their sides, guarding their "babies". If there was anything humorous about fusing the bombs, it was being able to see some of the drawings and slogans that the armorers had scrawled on the bombs with chalk or paint. Drawings of Hitler with bombs falling on him, or things like, "Hope you like this one, Adolph!" had adorned several of the bombs. Although the ground crews were safe during the missions over Europe, this was one way that they felt involved. *Their* bombs were being dropped, and they wanted to make it personal.

Aircraft assignment was another area of superstition among the bomber crews. Individual aircraft were cussed and discussed. Some planes seemed to lead a charmed life and seemed invincible. Others were deemed as death traps, waiting to kill a crew. Sometimes there might be a legitimate reason for this. Detroit pumps out millions of cars, and now and then a lemon hits the roads. Aircraft production was cranking out planes at the rate of hundreds a day, all over the United States. Manufacturers who had been building those cars were now building Army trucks, tanks, and aircraft. Now and then maybe a lemon of an airplane or tank was produced, but most of the aircraft branded as inferior were the product of after-mission scuttlebutt that made these legends grow into airfield folklore. If an aircraft came back time after time from bad missions, shot full of holes, but making it home just the same, it would become a "good" plane. If planes were losing engines, oxygen systems failing, etc, they became known as trying to kill you, and were met with scorn by the crew assigned to it.

Pragmatically, most "normal" people would see an aircraft as a collection of mechanical parts that were assembled in such a way as to make it fly and perform its role in taking the war to the enemy. It did not think, breathe, or care what was happening to it. It was the crew's job to make it work the way it was designed to do. But pilots weren't "normal" people, nor were their crews. Despite trying to be realistic about it, flight crews often became caught up in the folklore and superstition, and like mentioned before, many of the crew members carried their good luck charms and talismans and hoped for a "good" airplane to be assigned to them on mission day. As aviators have said for decades, sometimes it's better to be lucky than good.

Usually the crews were named for their pilot. The Fowler crew was named after 2nd Lieutenant James F. Fowler from Marion, South Carolina. He was the man flying the left seat as the pilot. On today's mission he was twenty-two-years-old, and the U.S. Army Air Force had deemed him as suitable for commanding the crew of nine men who were flying with him, and entrusted him with the 68,000lb aircraft and all the weapons that it carried. They were ordering him to take his men under his wing (literally), and fly them to Frankfurt, Germany and unload 6,000lbs of bombs on a target. But when he and his crew arrived at their assigned aircraft, #42-39786, he didn't say anything to show his disappointment, for that would not have befitted the image of a good aircraft commander. But he didn't have to say anything, because most of his crew had more than enough to say to make up for his silence.

Serial number 42-39786 was a B-17G-1-VE that was built in Burbank, California by the Lockheed Vega assembly plant. Although Boeing designed the B-17, the demand for the aircraft was high, and other companies were contracted to help build them in order to meet the delivery quotas. Douglas and Lockheed were competitors of Boeing, but both were building the B-17. Under the wartime construction mandates to build aircraft as quickly as possible, this was not unusual.

The Lockheed Vega division built 2,750 B-17s under license from Boeing during the war, and along with the Fowler crew's 42-39786, two other B-17G models came off the line consecutively with it. Sister ships 42-39785 and 42-39787 rolled out the door before and after 42-39786, and all three were destined to go to the 303rd Bomb Group at Molesworth.

The three bombers left the factory in late August, and after the installation of electronics, calibration of the guns, and a final inspection, they were deemed completed and ready for the long delivery flight across the United States and the North Atlantic. The three bombers arrived at RAF Molesworth on October 18, 1943, with 42-38786 going to the 427th Squadron, and the other two aircraft going to the 358th Squadron.

As I was writing one of the final drafts of this book, I found myself very interested in the status of the "mystery plane", serial number 42-39787, one of the "sister" B-17G's that came off the Lockheed Vega production line in Burbank, California. This aircraft, along with 42-39786 and 42-39785, were all delivered to the 303rd Bomb Group at Molesworth at the same time. 42-39786 went to the 427th Squadron and became named *G.I. Sheets*. 42-39785 was assigned to the 358th Squadron and became named *Thru Hel'en Hiwater*. 42-39787 was also assigned to the 358th Squadron, but its status was very murky.

According to the official Air Force records, which I obtained from Air Force headquarters at Maxwell Air Force Base, 42-39787 *was* returned to the States, but the date that occurred is unreadable on the copy of the aircraft's official history card. Elsewhere there was a date that it was pulled from service and returned to Air Training Command in January of 1944. It's also interesting that the official history of 42-39787 is recorded on an entirely different type of card than the two sister aircraft when all three rolled out of the factory at the same time, all three being delivered to the same field in the U.K. Another troubling factor is that both 42-39785 and 42-39787 went to the 358th Squadron, but -787's history was so different that -785.

And to add to the mystery...B-17 #42-39787 was recorded by the 358th Squadron as having five different names: *Wanton Woman, Watch*

Woman, War Bride, Wonton Woman, and *Old Faithful.* It's not unusual for an aircraft to be renamed, especially if it's survived many missions over several months, so this might be a simple case of lousy bookkeeping by the clerks in the 358th But one must admit that there's a lot of strange situations involving one particular B-17. And to top it off, 42-39787, who supposedly had five names, was listed by the 358th as both a -G model and an -F model at different times. All three of these bombers were definitely -G models.

She either flew lots of missions under different names, or she came back to the States in January '44 and flew with Air Training Command in Oklahoma and Texas before going on the scrapyard in Walnut Ridge, Arkansas after the war. She should have had a sixth name: *The Mystery Woman.*

In looking at the individual bombing mission reports, it can be seen that this aircraft actually flew more than five missions, and also carried two other names. The records on it are confusing, but it officially went to Air Training Command very early in a bombing campaign that needed every aircraft it could muster. It is definitely an aircraft that had a curious existence, and later in this book there will be a discussion of why this possibly took place.

For this mission to Frankfurt on January 29, 1944, the Fowler crew had been assigned to 42-39826, now named "*G.I. Sheets*". The original crew that had named the aircraft was commanded by pilot Captain Robert Sheets, and the name of the plane was an adaptation of his name and alluded to the gastrointestinal problem of loose bowels commonly known by military men as "the G.I. shits". It was fitting that the plane was liked about as much as the malady that it was named after. Several crews had flown the airplane, and most had experienced problems with it. One crew had missed a mission because one engine failed to start. It also had the reputation of being tedious to fly in formation because it seemed to be "out of rig", meaning that it felt as if the flight controls were out of balance. Co-pilot Barney Rawlings had told the author that he approached the aircraft that morning with a larger sense of dread than usual.

One negative aspect of the bomber assigned to the Fowler crew had nothing to do with this one in particular, but was because it was a "G" model. Most of the B-17s flown by the 303rd Bomb Group were B-17F and B-17G models. The "G" was a newer and supposedly improved version, but one of the improvements had caused a problem that wasn't anticipated by the designers.

The B-17G had an additional "chin" gun turret that was installed below the plexiglass-covered nose compartment where the bombardier and navigator stations were. The two additional .50 caliber guns gave additional protection from head-on attacks that the German fighter pilots favored, but the turret caused a great deal of aerodynamic drag. The "G" was much slower for a given engine power setting than the "F" model, and this caused the "G" model to have to run its engines at higher power settings to maintain formation with the "F" models. Running the engines faster burned more fuel, which meant they had to carry more fuel. Carrying more fuel meant more weight, which meant a longer, more dangerous takeoff roll, a slower climb, and poor handling qualities while trying to maintain position in formation. The fuel load for this 6.5 hour mission to Frankfurt and back for the B-17F was 2,100 gallons, but 2,400 gallons for the "G". That meant that the B-17G had to carry an extra 1,800 lbs of weight in fuel just because of the chin turret in the nose.

In the "after action" reports that were done after each mission, pilots and engineers all complained about the mixing of the two models in formations, and recommended that if it had to be done, have the lead crews (the lead aircraft in each element of the formation) fly the "G" models, and have the "F" models follow. The thought that it was easier for the "F" models to slow down rather than the "G" models to speed up made sense, but like much in the military, no one in the command structure who could make that decision ever agreed with the complaints of the crews, so the B-17G's were always run hard and overworked. Logic wasn't always operative in the military, it seems.

Logic aside, the members of the Fowler crew accepted their aircraft assignment, basically because that was all that they could do. Somebody had to fly *G.I. Sheets*, and today it was their responsibility. They accepted the hand they were dealt. They'd ridden this temperamental beast into battle before, and like it or not, they'd do it again today.

chapter two

THE CREW

Despite their misfortune in drawing the *G.I. Sheets* as their assigned aircraft, the members of the Fowler crew set about preparing themselves and the big bomber for the mission. As mentioned earlier, the bombardier, 2nd Lieutenant Alvin L. Taylor, was one of the first to arrive at the plane and had installed the bombsight and fused the bombs. Now he sat on his stool behind the bombsight, his legs stretched out before him and a sheaf of photos and maps on his lap. He studied the photos of their target, which happened to be a factory in Frankfurt. He would have to visually see the target in order to drop bombs accurately, but if the target was obscured by clouds, they would drop when signaled to do so by a pathfinder aircraft. The pathfinder used a rudimentary radio direction finding system to "guess" at where the target was, and would signal elements of the formation to drop. The accuracy certainly wasn't guaranteed, but with as many bombs as would be falling, some would hit the target.

Taylor, a stocky 23-year-old Texan, was on his eighth mission, but nothing had become routine about what he was doing. Every mission was a bit different because each target required different procedures. Mission planners used reconnaissance photos to plan on how best to approach a target. The navigation from England to the area near the target was fairly straight forward, but somewhere just short of the target was a landmark that was designated as the "initial point", or "I.P." All aircraft would go to their assigned I.P., then turn to a specific compass heading to travel the last few miles to the target. The bombardier's job basically started just before reaching the I.P. His first task was to identify the I.P. through his bombsight, then give the pilot the compass heading to fly toward the target. From what he had seen on the target photos, he would know how far he was from the target and give the pilot corrections in order to stay on course toward the drop point. If he were the lead bombardier, or if he had to bomb the target on his own and not with the formation, he would actually take control of the aircraft from the pilot and would be able to control the bomber's heading as it approached the target. After putting in wind speed and direction, the speed of the plane, and the altitude, the bombsight would compute the point at which to drop the bomb in order for it to hit the target. On today's mission, he was bombing with the lead bombardier of his element. When he saw that bombardier release bombs, he would follow suit. Taylor's job today would be easy, if everything went as planned, but all the bombardiers in an element of the formation had to be prepared to plan and execute the actual drop in case there was a problem with the lead bombardier. Taylor would also have the navigator in his aircraft as a back up to help him locate the I.P. and double check the approach to the target.

2nd Lieutenant Joseph Thompson, 28, also a Texan, had just climbed into the nose compartment and was putting his charts, plotters, and pencils on his small map desk off the side and behind Taylor's position. Like Taylor, his job was to be prepared to take over navigation if for some reason their plane became separated from the formation. Since they were in a long formation of bombers headed to Frankfurt, today's mission was basically a follow-the-leader affair, so it should be simple.

But the navigator's job was very important for another reason. In spite of the fact that navigation to and from the target was easy enough if everything went as planned, the navigator had to keep track of their current location continually in the event there was a problem that resulted in his plane being separated from the formation. He had to know where he was at all times in order to know how to proceed to wherever they had to go if a course change was necessary.

The jobs of the navigator and the bombardier overlapped somewhat in the performance of their duties, and the Army Air Force did pursue cross training both occupations in each area. The only problem with this was the lack of training facilities and qualified instructors. The overcrowding at the schools that trained both navigators and bombardiers precluded putting more trainees in the training facilities, and the shortage of instructors made the building and staffing of more schools a problem. The dual training of these crewmen was sporadic, so some navigators and bombardiers had training in both skills, some did not. By the time of this mission, most of the men trained during late 1942 to mid-1943 were trained in both skills, but were officially titled either "navigator" or "bombardier". In late 1944 and early 1945, with the advent of the B-29 in the Pacific war with the Japanese, almost all were trained in both areas and were classified as "bombardier/navigator", regardless of which position they filled on the big bomber.

Thompson's presence on today's mission proved something of a mystery. He arrived in England with the other members of the Fowler crew in early November 1943, and flew as navigator with the Humphreys crew on a mission on December 6th. Inexplicably, he did not fly any further missions until January 21, 1944, the first with the Fowler crew to which he was assigned.

Today's mission to Frankfurt would be his third mission, while most of his fellow crewmen were flying their eighth or ninth. Thompson's early mission and his absence from other missions for nearly three months were never explained. The only reference to his absence was found in a quote he had given in the Missing Air Crew Report (MACR) in late 1944 when he stated that he was not familiar with certain information because he "had been hospitalized at that time". There was no explanation given for that statement, or what it referred to, but it covered a time period when his fellow crewmen were flying missions, and he apparently was not on flight status.

Another crew member who had arrived at the plane before the rest of the crew was engineer Curtis Finley, from Nebraska. Finley's job entailed knowing everything about the B-17 that they were flying. He did not perform maintenance and was not a mechanic, but he was responsible with knowing that everything was in tiptop shape with the bomber before and during the mission. He was also responsible with reporting any defects and battle damage to the maintenance staff upon the return from a mission. Finley had given the *G.I. Sheets* a thorough inspection that morning and had started all the engines to warm the oil. After warming the engines and making sure there were no apparent problems, he shut them down.

After shutting down the engines, a fuel truck, one of several patrolling the perimeter track around the airfield, stopped to replenish the fuel used in the engine test. For today's mission, they would need their maximum allowed load of fuel. Finley was the only man on the crew who was a career military man, having been a soldier since before Pearl Harbor. In about a week he would turn thirty, making him the second oldest man on the Fowler crew. In addition to being the engineer, he was also the top turret gunner.

Finley reported to pilot James Fowler that he'd found nothing wrong with their assigned aircraft. Fowler settled himself in the left seat and stowed his gear. His copilot, 2nd Lieutenant Bernard "Barney" Rawlings, did the same in the seat to his right. Rawlings was a tall 23-year-old from Kansas City, Missouri. Unlike Fowler, who was new to piloting until the Air Force had trained him, Rawlings had worked for Trans World Airlines before the war in a ground job but had taken flying lessons in hope of one day flying for the airline.

Just because he was familiar to flying made no difference to the Air Force, and he still had to go through the year-long training program to go from fledgling pilot to second-in-command on the huge bomber. The training that he and Fowler had endured was the longest and most intense of anyone on the crew, moving to one field for primary training, another for basic training (formation, night, and instrument flying), and to yet another field for advanced training in multi-engine aircraft. After that, it was off to finally two more airfields for specialized B-17 bomber training. To become an Air Force pilot, the selection and training was grueling, and many did not make the cut.

Of the enlisted crewmen, Technical Sergeant Donald Dinwiddie, the radioman, was the most highly trained crewman in the most demanding position. Dinwiddie was the youngest member of the crew, just short of his twenty-first birthday, which was coming up in less than two months. Like Rawlings, he was a Missourian, born and raised in the small community of Higbee. Higbee was in the central part of the state, just northeast of Columbia. Dinwiddie gave up a job in a Remington Arms Company factory in Kansas City to enlist in the Air Force. He was a machinist in the arms factory making rifles for the war, and would've been safe from being drafted. However, like many young men of his age, he felt the need to serve his country in a more direct way. Making M-1 rifles was necessary for the war, but dropping bombs on the enemy was a more personal way to fight the Germans and the Japanese. Besides, serving in the military was in his family; his brother Tyree was serving in the Army in the Pacific, his brother Archie was a pharmacist's mate in the Navy in the Atlantic Fleet, and his brother Jack was a 2nd lieutenant in the Army. On November 6, 1942, Don Dinwiddie enlisted in the U.S. Army Air Force at Fort Leavenworth, Kansas.

After taking the military aptitude tests during basic military training in Texas, Dinwiddie was deemed academically talented enough to be put into radio school. Radio operators not only had to learn Morse code in order to send and receive twenty words a minute with all the dots and dashes, but they also had to know how a radio worked. During training, they had to actually take what they learned about radio theory and build a working radio from parts. The intent of that training was to enable them to fix a malfunctioning radio on a mission if the situation demanded. After basic military training in Texas, he was sent to Truax Field in Madison, Wisconsin for the grueling radio training.

After finishing the twenty-week radio school, he then had to train as a gunner. Radiomen on the B-17 also had a machine gun in their compartment, and when encountering attacks by enemy fighter planes, the radioman was pressed into service to man a gun that fired up and toward the rear of the bomber. The B-17 carried at least ten machine guns, some models had thirteen, and all the crewmen except the pilot and copilot received gunnery training. After graduating from radio school in Wisconsin, Dinwiddie then traveled to the desolate Wendover Field in Utah. Like most of the students arriving there, he was struck by the intensity of it all. There, on a mountainside overlooking the field in the Utah desert, was a huge sign made of white letters, looking much like the famous "Hollywood" sign in Los Angeles. This sign was a little more ominous, however, and it was a stark introduction to the world they were entering. The letters spelled out "*KILL OR BE KILLED*". After seeing the shocking letters, the students were surprised to find that one of the first weapons on which they would be trained were BB guns. But the BB guns used in gunnery school were a little different than what most of them had as kids. They were fired by compressed air and shot continuously as long as you held the trigger down. These "BB machine guns" were used to learn how to track moving targets. Another training contraption was borrowed from the carnival—a conveyor belt moving small profile models of enemy aircraft were shot at with .22 rifles, again used to learn to track and lead targets. From the .22 rifles and BB guns, the gunnery students were trained with shotguns on a skeet range. Again, learning to track and shoot a clay bird was remarkably similar to tracking and shooting at a fast-moving enemy fighter.

After such training, student gunners were then introduced to the .30 caliber and the heavier .50 caliber machine guns that they'd find on the B-17s. The .30 caliber light machine gun was found on in the radioman's compartment on earlier models of the B-17, as well as the left and right nose guns operated by the navigator and bombardier. The .50 caliber was used in the top turret (two guns mounted side by side), the ball turret on the bottom of the plane (also two side by side), the tail gun (two side by side), and the right and left waist gun ports (a single gun at each position). Before the gunnery training was over, successful students were able to fire all the weapons accurately, and were able to dismantle and reassemble any of the guns while blindfolded and wearing gloves. Why were they tested wearing the blindfolds and gloves? It was to try to simulate the real conditions in which they would be working.

At the high altitudes at which they would be flying, it was not unusual for the gunner's goggles to fog over, and the below-freezing temperatures would cause frostbite and skin would freeze to the gun if gloves weren't worn. The training tried to prepare the crewmen for all possibilities. In addition, all gunnery students were tested on firing at moving target panels pulled by tow aircraft.

These targets would be towed past a bomber manned by students and their instructors. The only bad thing about shooting at these targets was that one important detail was lacking: the targets weren't firing back at you like a Messerschmitt or Focke Wulf. No matter how thorough the training, nothing was like actual combat.

After successfully completing gunnery training, Technical Sergeant Dinwiddie had one more job to learn. In addition to being a radio operator and gunner, he was also trained as the medic for the bomber, the crewman who would try to render aid to any of the men that could be helped if wounded. The radioman was responsible for many things in the operation of the bomber, but his main job was that of maintaining communication with the lead plane of the group from Molesworth. From takeoff until return to the field after the mission, his job was to listen to his radios for any messages from the higher commands of the 8th Air Force or Division Headquarters in the event of a deviation in plans for the mission. He also had to work with the bombardier and navigator in order to know where they were and when to broadcast position reports, if necessary. He also had to maintain a log of all transmissions he sent and messages he received. One of the most important aspects of his job was that he was in possession of the daily mission codes. These codes were used to validate the authenticity of any orders that came from 8th Air Force. The Germans had been known to broadcast false commands in order to foul up missions, so the coded validations were necessary in order to assure their legitimacy. Like the Norden bombsight, these codes, although only good for the day of the mission, had to be destroyed if the aircraft was forced down.

The radioman's duties were varied, and so was his equipment. His compartment was in the central part of the aircraft, just behind the bomb bay. In his compartment he had both Morse code and voice transmitters and a couple of different receivers in order to communicate with other aircraft and land bases. He also had some basic instrumentation such as an altimeter, a compass, a clock, and an outside air temperature indicator. These would enable him to help the navigator and pilots in making position reports.

The radio operator's logs were also a backup in case the navigator was put out of commission and the pilots had to navigate on their own. The radio operator had many more duties than just operating the radios.

Despite all the duties that fell on Dinwiddie, there was an upside to the job of radioman: the radio compartment was roomy and heated.

Excluding the pilot and copilot, it can be seen that the navigator, bombardier, engineer, and radioman were also gunners in addition to their primary duties. But there were four crewmen who were dedicated to the mission of defending the bomber against enemy fighters. These men were primarily gunners but were often cross-trained in other jobs as well and could help out if necessary. These gunners had the most environmentally difficult jobs on the bomber.

Staff Sergeant Richard Arrington was a twenty-three year-old from New Orleans, Louisiana. He was short in stature, which was a requirement for his job on board the bomber. He was the ball turret gunner, manning the Sperry ball turret located on the aft underside of the B-17. The ball turret was a spherical compartment that was electrically-powered and could swing its twin .50 caliber machine guns in a 360 degree circle as well as up and down. When operating correctly, it added a remarkable defensive position to the B-17.

Arrington had to crawl into the ball after the aircraft was airborne. He would enter through a hatch and would fly the entire mission in almost in a fetal position, the rear of his guns almost in his face, and the barrels of the guns firing from between his knees. He was able to swing, elevate, and fire the Brownings using buttons on the gun's grips. If Arrington's ball became inoperative for any reason, he could be trapped in the turret until someone could manually roll it around in order for him to crawl out of the hatch and return to the fuselage of the bomber. If left in the turret until after the landing, all Arrington could do was pray that the bomber didn't have to make a wheel's up landing. In that case, the full weight of the bomber would crush the turret and Arrington. A jammed turret could be accessed from inside the bomber, but it was not an easy job. It would take about twenty minutes using the proper tools to rotate the ball and extricate the gunner. There were all kinds of bad scenarios that could befall the ball turret gunner. It was not a job for the claustrophobic or one who dwelt too much about the "what if".

Another gun position requiring the proper mental and physical abilities was that of the tail gunner. Like the name says, the tail gun position was at the tip of the back of the plane, under the big vertical stabilizer and rudder. The tail gunner would get into his compartment by crawling through the rear of the fuselage and straddling a small seat that enabled him to be in a kneeling/sitting position with his head sticking up into a plexiglass enclosure. His twin Browning .50 caliber guns could be swung up and down and left and right, and his job was to watch for aircraft attacking from the rear and firing on them when they came in range. The tail of any bomber was vulnerable to attack, but the tail guns of a B-17 were deadly, and the German pilots thought twice about attacking directly toward the tail. Staff Sergeant Jack Ferguson was the tail gunner on today's mission to Frankfurt. Ferguson's position was almost, but not quite, as physically demanding as the ball turret. He could get out of his position and squirm through the tail back into the main part of the fuselage, and usually did so when flying back home from a mission after the threat of enemy fighters disappeared. Ferguson didn't consider himself as a full-fledged member of the Fowler crew. He had flown several missions with them, but was there as a replacement for a missing tail gunner.

Staff Sergeant Harry Wallrobenstein had been the original tail gunner for the Fowler crew, but had disappeared after a mission to Bremen, Germany flown on December 13, 1943. By all indications it was a routine mission, but the skies had been cloudy, and the bombing results were only fair due to the target being obscured. There had been no enemy fighter opposition, and very little antiaircraft fire. Back on the ground at Molesworth after the mission, Wallrobenstein and his friend Don Dinwiddie were walking around the bomber looking for flak damage. They discovered that an unexploded antiaircraft shell had gone through one side of the fuselage and out the other side, just behind the head of Wallrobenstein, and he was visibly shaken. "Don", he exclaimed, "I think those bastards were trying to kill me!" That was the last time that anyone on the Fowler crew saw him. His disappearance remained a mystery for years.

Wallrobenstein was a thirty year-old from Pittsburgh, and it would be several years before his mysterious disappearance would be solved. In the meantime, Ferguson, a twenty-three year-old from California, had served with the Fowler crew on several missions, but he saw himself as a temporary replacement and never felt as if he were part of the "family" that had been together since back in the States.

The other two gunners were manning the waist guns. Staff Sergeants Loren Zimmer, a twenty-three year-old Nebraskan, and Miller Jackson, 38, from Alabama, fired out of large openings in the left and right sides of the aft fuselage. Their guns were fitted to flexible mounts that enabled them to be moved up and down and left and right, giving them a wide range of movement and firing area. The bad part of their job was that the openings that they fired though filled the entire aft of the fuselage with a frigid blast of air. To combat the cold, they wore layers of bulky clothing plus their flak vests. The waist gunners had to stand at their firing positions for most of the mission. In addition to the cold, standing at the gun ports became a problem in a busy gunfight because of the empty shell casings that collected on the floor. The bulky boots and the brass "empties" made it feel as slippery as ice, and the gunners would have to sweep the shells away with their feet until there was a lull in the action long enough to do a better clean-up.

In discussing gunners and their ammunition, it should be noted that there was a standard loading of ammunition allowed for each mission. Some gunners and crews became ammo hoarders, trying to save back ammo from a mission in order to be used on the coming missions. It was all supposed to be turned in, but sometimes not all of it made it back to the armory. The simple truth was that there was no way to accurately predict the fighter opposition, so why trust the mission planners to tell you how much ammo you'd need? The weight of the bomb load, fuel load, and ammo load was always factored into computing the takeoff gross weight of the bomber. A good pilot always planned on a bit more weight than official paperwork indicated…how much depended on the resourcefulness of his gunners.

With the exception of tail gunner Jack Ferguson, the Fowler crew had been together since the late summer of 1943. All of them had successfully completed mastering their individual skills, and it culminated in each of them being assigned to B-17 crew training in Texas. All of them had received orders to Pyote Field, near Odessa, Texas. In this phase of training, their individual skills coalesced to form a team that would fly as a unit in order to take the bomber into combat. Basically, the training at Pyote was to get used to the bomber and each other. Pyote wasn't a pleasant place to be. Nicknamed "Rattlesnake Field" for a good reason, it was hot, snake-infested, and resembled nothing that should be a part of training to bomb the Germans.

Soon enough they had progressed to the point of flying the bomber as a team, each doing the jobs that they had been trained to do, and they were ready for combat transition training at Dyersburg Field, Tennessee.

Dyersburg was just across the Mississippi River separating Tennessee from Arkansas, and was a very active training field.

Training at Dyersburg was as close to actual combat as the Air Training Command could muster. Of course, there were no enemy planes shooting at them, but they flew in all kinds of weather, flew long distances, and flew at night. Everything was done in formation with other bombers. The B-17, with all of its guns, was still no match for a flight of German fighters if it were by itself, but in a formation with other B-17's, enemy pilots thought twice about attacking. To make the training at Dyersburg as realistic as possible, even the streets on the field had British names, and the airfield itself had a British nickname: "Peterborough". The idea was to get the green crews to start thinking of what they were soon going to be doing in a land completely different than the one in which they had grown up and lived in all of their lives.

For Don Dinwiddie, little did he know that when he was assigned to Dyersburg, he was going to be just a few miles from where he would spend a great deal time later in his life. Cape Girardeau, Missouri was only about sixty air miles from Dyersburg, and he'd move there with his family in October of 1961.

Soon the training at Dyersburg came to an end. It marked the end of all of their training, and they were soon bound for England. Some crews were often assigned to pick up bombers new from the factory and deliver them to England, but the Fowler crew, like most, were not that lucky. As a crew, they traveled together to New York and boarded the former luxury ocean liner Queen Elizabeth for the cruise to Britain. Unlike its previous life, the ship had been converted to carry troops, not wealthy passengers, and they were packed into the vessel like sardines in order to make the best use of its massive space.

The voyage over the North Atlantic certainly wasn't a pleasure cruise. The troops were restricted in their movement about the ship and were not allowed free access except to certain areas. They were not allowed out on the decks except for very short times. Being outside on the decks wasn't a pleasant experience anyway. This was the North Atlantic, and late fall, nearing winter, and the weather was bitter. Keeping the passengers restricted to certain areas was also part of the disaster control program.

At this point in the war, late 1943, German submarines routinely stalked the Atlantic shipping lanes, and there was a very real possibility of being torpedoed while making the crossing. The troops on board were routinely drilled on lifeboat access and deployment and damage control exercises. The ship seldom traveled very far in a straight line, and periodically changed course, zigzagging its way across the Atlantic to England. The purpose of the evasive maneuvers was to make it more difficult for a lurking U-boat to aim it's torpedoes at the large vessel. The crossing from New York to England was the first taste of the war in which the young men would soon be immersed.

The ship finally made its way to their destination in the United Kingdom, coming into port in Glasgow, Scotland on November 9, 1943.

The first several days in Britain saw them in a replacement depot, awaiting assignment. After about a week, the Fowler crew was assigned to the 427th Squadron of the 303rd Bomb Group of the 41st Combat Wing of the First Bombardment Division of the Eighth Air Force. What that mouthful meant was that they were going to one of the many airfields in England where American aircraft were based. Their particular field was the former Royal Air Force installation at Molesworth. RAF Molesworth, like many other British airfields, was given over to the U.S. Army Air Force in order to make room for the very large (and very welcomed) bomber force that the Americans were sending to war. At this point in the war, the 303rd Bomb Group consisted of four squadrons of roughly ten planes each. The squadrons were the 358th, 359th, 360th, and the 427th. The field had two runways, the longest one lengthened and reinforced in order to handle the heavier American bombers. It was one of over one hundred bases that were home to the B-17 and B-24 bombers of the U.S. Eighth Air Force. The "Mighty Eighth" was not only home to the big four-engine bombers, but also possessed the light and medium bombers like the B-25 and B-26, and the P-51s, P-47s, and P-38s that flew as escorts to defend bomber formations into and out of German-occupied Europe.

After the attack on Pearl Harbor, during the early part of the direct involvement of the United States in the war, daylight bombing was an experiment that was always on the edge of failure. The bombers, even though they bristled with several defensive machine guns, were no match for the Luftwaffe pilots and planes that had been battle tested since 1939. Only in massed formation could they effectively defend themselves.

The United States was woefully unprepared for war, and suddenly found itself fighting on two sides of the globe against both the Germans and the Japanese. The U.S. bomber doctrine was to strategically destroy selected factories, refineries, airfields, transportation hubs, trains, railroads, ports, etc. In short, the plan was to destroy anything that would aid in preventing the enemy from mobilizing an attempt to expand its hold on occupied territory. Secondarily, the bombing would hopefully be successful in softening up Western Europe for a ground invasion by Allied forces which would drive the Germans out of the countries that they had seized and occupied, hopefully resulting in their defeat.

One definitive weapon the United States possessed wasn't something concrete…it was an ideal. Freedom had been the cornerstone of our country, a country founded by individuals who were not afraid to fight to defend it. Before the U.S. entered the war, Americans were already involved. Some had already joined the fight by enlisting in the Royal Canadian Air Force or the Royal Air Force, despite laws in the United States that forbade it. Later, after the United States came into the war, these Canadian and British enlistees were moved into the American Air Force. When the Japanese attacked Pearl Harbor, recruiting stations were swamped with men wanting to enlist. Some joined the army, navy, or marines by their choice, and accepted any job assigned to them. Some young men such as Don Dinwiddie and the others on the Fowler crew, officers and enlisted men alike, were unique.

Being an aviator, whether pilot, bombardier, navigator, radioman, or gunner, meant that they were all volunteers. Nobody was forced to fly as long as there were volunteers who wanted the job. Just like the sailors who volunteered for submarine duty, it took a special person who wanted to be an aviator, but there was no shortage of them. The mental and physical demands were tough, and many who wanted to serve as an aircrew member didn't get accepted or made it through the rigorous training.

After a train trip from Scotland to Cambridge, the Fowler crew arrived at RAF Molesworth in November 1943 and were soon sporting the flight jacket patch denoting the 427th Squadron—Bugs Bunny, jauntily standing with one foot on a bomb. Like most aviation units, each squadron had its own insignia, often a familiar cartoon character. Walt Disney Studios and Warner Brothers both helped design some of the more memorable insignia.

It wasn't unusual to see Felix the Cat, Donald Duck, Mickey Mouse, etc, going off to war on a flight jacket or painted on the nose of an aircraft. The entertainment industry in general tried to contribute to the war effort and morale-building of the troops. Hollywood saw many of its stars involved in U.S.O. tours, acting in training films, and participating in war bond drives, but some took a more active role in the actual fighting. Clark Gable, a huge star at the time, actually went on missions with the 303rd in order to film a short feature about the bombing missions out of England and to show the American people back home what it was like to be a bomber crew member.

He received training as an aerial gunner and participated in several missions. Gable was actually a captain in the U.S. Army Air Force and tasked with making documentaries, but chose to enter combat to get the true experience.

Probably the most notable Hollywood celebrity involved in the war was Jimmy Stewart. Stewart was not in the war to do anything for Hollywood or to make documentaries. He was the real deal, giving up movie-making and stardom in order to be a bomber pilot. Tall and lanky, he was first rejected from the service because he was underweight. After several days of heavy eating, he retook the physical was accepted after he had gained a few pounds. Stewart was already a civilian pilot and was so skilled that the air force waived some of his military training. After he received his military wings, he was made an instructor, which upset him very much. As he was working as a multi-engine instructor, he kept applying for combat duty, and finally was accepted. It seems that Hollywood was petitioning the military to keep him safe because of his film career. Stewart basically gave up acting indefinitely for the war effort, and vowed he'd stay out of the movie industry permanently if he didn't get to do his part for the war. His primary role, he felt, was as a full-fledged combat pilot, not as an instructor. The Hollywood executives who were trying to protect him finally relented, and he flew both the B-17 and B-24 out of England on every mission he could fly. He ended the war as the deputy commander of the Second Bombardment Division with the rank of full colonel. He remained in the Air Force Reserve after the war and retired as a brigadier general. Stewart was also a very active civilian pilot after the war and owned and flew several different aircraft over the years. He and his wife often flew from California back east to visit his family in Pennsylvania.

The first bombing missions were flown by the 303rd out of Molesworth the year before the Fowler crew arrived. The first daylight bombing missions flown by the U.S. Army Air Force were either very easy "milk runs" or incredibly disastrous with horrendous losses in men and aircraft. The problem was that it had never been done before, and the Americans were trying to learn how to go about bombing the Germans, and the Germans were, at the same time, trying to figure out how to best defend themselves. The scales would often tip in one direction or the other, but the trend began to very slowly turn in favor of the Allies.

It cannot be overstated that what was going on early in the war was totally new and a necessary experiment. The only Allied offensive against Germany was the air war. The bomber commanders of both the U.S. Army Air Force and the Royal Air Force were writing the book on how to do it *as* they did it.

Hitler had initiated his conquest of Europe on September 1, 1939 when his troops invaded Poland. Just shortly a year later, most of Continental Europe was occupied by the Nazis. Until the Allied invasion of Normandy on June 6, 1944, there was no ground war being fought other than in North Africa and Italy. For over four years the Germans had a stranglehold on most of Europe, and it's an amazing fact that after the D-Day invasion, the ground war was relatively short, with the Germans surrendering less than a year later. The American air war of strategic bombing began in 1942, softening up the German hold on Western Europe and denying the enemy access to fuel, manufacturing facilities, and transportation. Without aerial bombardment, the war would have taken much longer to prosecute, and many more lives would have been lost in the prolonged ground offensive.

By November of 1943, when Don Dinwiddie and his crewmates arrived on the scene, the missions were no less brutal, but conditions were much improved on many levels. Things like proper grease that didn't gum up the machine guns in the frigid temperatures at high altitude, electrically heated flying suits that didn't catch fire as often, better oxygen masks, and the biggest thing of all, fighter escorts all the way into Germany, came on the scene.

Fighter escorts had always been effective to keep the German fighters at bay, but the problem was that the long range bombers could go deeper into Europe to bomb, but fighters, with their smaller fuel capacity, couldn't fly as far.

The invention of the disposable drop tank solved that problem. Made of lightweight, but very strong compressed paper, the drop tank would hold nearly one hundred gallons of fuel long enough for a couple of hours of flying. The escort pilots would burn off the fuel from the drop tanks first, then switch to the main tanks. The tanks were cost-effective and also enabled the fighters to stay airborne for enough time to give coverage over the entire route into and out of Germany. The disposable drop tank was one of those unusual items, born out of necessity, that made a huge difference in how the air war was able to be effectively fought.

By the time the Fowler crew came to England, the 303rd and other bomb groups were at the high point of the bombing campaign. The round-the-clock pounding of the Germans by the Americans in the day and the British at night was having a marked effect on the enemy.

Airfields, factories, railroads, ports, and refineries were being destroyed by the Allies faster than the Germans could rebuild them. The enemy was being slowly strangled, paving the way for the ground invasion that would be coming in the future. Not all of the missions were successful, but the majority were favorable to the Allies.

Like all the young men that arrived in England, the Fowler crew was ready to get in the fight. Unfortunately, after all the training that they'd endured in the States, they had more training to do in England. Part of it was just getting used to the strange environment. The old saying that the "Americans and the British were a people separated by a common language" was certainly true. The first thing to learn was what they should and should not do, and how not to offend their British cousins. They had to figure out the silly English money, and they were shocked that the Brits drank their beer *warm*.

The British often described the Yanks who had suddenly taken over their countryside as "overpaid, oversexed, and over here", and they may have given the impression that they didn't like the Americans being there in such large numbers, but the vast majority felt otherwise. Without the presence of the Americans, the Germans would have been there instead. So, if not openly welcomed, the American soldiers were tolerated. It must be remembered that at this point in time, it wasn't just the American aviators in England. All over the British Isles, thousands of Allied ground troops were massed, training for the day that the ground invasion of occupied Europe would begin.

The Fowler crew found themselves getting rapidly immersed in English customs and the 303rd Bomb Group policies and procedures. Affecting the commissioned officers more than the enlisted crew, they found themselves learning the ropes of how the missions were flown. While the pilots were learning such things of takeoff and assembly procedures, use of local radio navigation stations, emergency landing field locations, and procedures for ditching a crippled bomber in the English Channel, the enlisted crew was being indoctrinated in some of the same things. Added to that list was identification of Allied and English aircraft. Since all of the enlisted crewmen were also gunners, it was important that they could all identify enemy aircraft and not confuse them with friendly planes. This point might seem insignificant, but in the excitement, fear, and fast pace of an air battle, it was easier than one might think to confuse an American P-51 with a Messerschmitt Me-109.

In fact, there were several cases of "friendly fire" from the gunners on the bombers damaging escorting fighters and wounding Allied pilots because of mistaken identity of the aircraft.

Because of incidents and accidents involving those crews who had come before them, training of crews new to the war used "real life" situations that could improve their chances for survival. Of particular interest was the training on escape and evasion in the event a crew had to bail out or were forced down over enemy territory.

Despite the hundreds of men who had been shot down over Europe, many had survived bailing out and had evaded capture by the Germans. There were various resistance organizations and underground groups that had developed effective networks in the Netherlands, Belgium, and France. Many airmen had made it back to England with their help. Airmen were taught what to expect, how to interact with these groups, and how to survive. Men who had evaded and escaped had stories to tell, and the new men listened.

After a few weeks of learning how things were done in England and in the 303rd, the Fowler crew made it into combat, albeit in a piecemeal fashion. After hanging out and hearing stories and explanations of how it was, some of the crew members were allowed to experience combat with other crews. As mentioned earlier, Lt. Joe Thompson flew a mission with another crew on December 5. The mission was to bomb targets in France, but was aborted due to weather before reaching the drop point.

On December 13, 1943, on a mission to Bremen, Germany, the rest of the Fowler crew flew their first combat mission. Fowler flew as pilot, but an experienced command pilot flew as his copilot instead of Barney Rawlings. An experienced navigator flew with the crew instead of Lt. Thompson. This was not an unusual situation for a new crew on their first mission.

Rawlings, not to be left out, wrangled a seat on *Vicious Virgin,* flown by the Robert Hullar crew. Rawlings flew not as a pilot, but as the tail gunner. The rationale was that anyone who could fly the B-17 should be able to handle the tail gun, and at the same time, he could act as a critical observer of the trailing formation.

Regardless of such postulation, Barney just wanted to fly the mission, and he didn't want to be left out when the rest of his crew was flying off into the war for which they'd all been trained.

The mission to Bremen, Germany was interesting, to be certain. The flak was heavy, but inaccurate, with only five aircraft receiving minor damage. One bomber had minor damage from friendly fire after being shot by a gunner on another B-17. There were no combat casualties on the mission except for the death of one gunner due to an oxygen system problem. Actual bombing accuracy was not great due to clouds covering most of the target area. But for the Fowler crew, it was a learning experience. By the end of the day on December 13, 1943, all of the Fowler crew were veterans of combat. Like a rite of passage, after that first combat mission and for every mission thereafter, there was a subtle change in their environment. Most crewmen didn't discuss it, but they all felt it.

After that first taste of air combat, there was a smell that was present inside every bomber they flew, noticeable as soon as they climbed aboard. Every bomber smelled the same, an amalgam of the aromas of fuel, gun grease, oil, cordite, and all too often, blood and vomit. The smells came together into a strong sensory reminder of combat... and fear. For some airmen, the pervasive smell in their memory would pull up other reminders of aerial combat: the noise of the engines, the pounding of the machine guns, the call on the intercom that a flight of fighters coming at them head-on. Sometimes all these smells, sounds and sights haunted their dreams, causing lack of sleep. For some crewmen, it kept them from flying. The polite term for it was "losing their nerve", and they often were pulled from flying because fear had made them useless and dangerous. Whether true or not, that could have been the reason navigator Joe Thompson had only flown the one mission early in December, and nothing more until late January. This is not said in order to label Thompson a coward. It was very common by this point in the bombing war for a crew member, officer or enlisted, to have to take a break from flying in order to get a grasp on his fears. The flak, the fighters, the unbearable cold, and the constant reminders of all that could kill you were hard to take for any succession of missions, much less twenty-five. Sometimes the crew member would withdraw from flying, other times one of the commanding officers would remove a crew member because of concerns that aviator's fear would cause problems for the rest of the crew.

chapter three

ON TO FRANKFURT

As the Fowler crew got settled into the *G.I. Sheets*, they had time to reflect on the importance of the day's mission to Frankfurt. It would be the largest mission thus far in the war. There would be nearly 1,000 bombers, including both B-17s and B-24s, taking off from fields all over Great Britain to gather in formation to fly in a long stream to Frankfurt. The aircraft would take off at designated times, fly individually to assembly points, then fly as a formation to join the stream at other predetermined points. The long formation of bombers would be of varying widths, stretching for over a distance of 360 miles. The length of the formation would be roughly the same as the distance from Wichita, Kansas to St. Louis, Missouri. After the first bomber released its bombs over the target, bombs would continue to rain down on Frankfurt for an hour and a half as each element of the long stream arrived over the targets. It would take that length of time for the last planes to arrive. Regardless of the actual physical damage on the chosen targets, the psychological damage would be monumental. This mission would send an unmistakable message to the Germans about what the Allies were capable of doing. At this stage in the war, the Germans still held all of Western Europe, but slowly the relentless bombing by the Allies had been doing its job to soften the enemy defenses so that the eventual ground invasion could be implemented. In post-war debriefings, high-ranking German officials said that seeing the thousands of Allied bombers that returned day and night to destroy their factories and military targets over and over sent a somber message about their chances of ever winning the war. The majority of them stated that they would have tried to arrange a surrender months before the war's actual end in an effort to save their country and their young soldiers, but the grip that Hitler had on them at the time was unbreakable, and his thoughts of winning the war were delusional.

At this point in the war, everyone knew that the round-the-clock bombing was doing its job, even at a high cost in lives and aircraft. As has been stated several times in this work, there was no ground war in Western Europe thus far, but it was common knowledge to Allies and Germans alike that it was inevitable.

Because of the difference in doctrine, the British Royal Air Force flew bombing missions at night, believing that daylight bombing was suicidal, resulting in little damage and the loss of many airmen. Their night bombing was radically different than the American daylight strategic bombing. Rather than dropping bombs on particular targets, they chose portions of cities to attack.

At dusk, small flights of very fast DeHavilland Mosquito fighter/bombers would depart England to attack parts of selected cities. Pinpoint accuracy wasn't important in putting incendiary bombs on the ground in order to start raging fires. The fires would rapidly spread, tying up firemen and equipment for hours. The fires would also become beacons and aiming points for the larger, heavier bombers that would depart England behind the Mosquitoes. British bombers did not fly in formation to the targets as the Americans did, but took off individually and flew in a string toward their destination. The RAF bombers flew a strict course to and from the targets at specific altitudes in order to not collide with one another. The British bombing campaign was not as successful strategically, but combined with the American daylight raids, it kept the enemy under constant attack, weather permitting. This gave the Germans little time to rebuild damage or prepare defensive weapons.

[Author's note: Had I been a pilot in World War II and could have had the privilege to choose my aircraft to fly, I would've picked the Mosquito. It was used in a multitude of roles during the war and excelled in all of them. There is a famous incident that occurred in the early days of the war that showed the Mosquito's utility and their pilots' skill. Hermann Goering, head of the German Luftwaffe, was giving a speech in Berlin that was being broadcast over radio. In the speech, just as he was telling the world that no bombs would ever fall on Berlin, explosions could be heard in the background. The explosions were from bombs being dropped by a flight of Mossies. Hollywood couldn't have scripted it any better!]

As the men of the *G.I. Sheets* and all the other crews sat in their bombers parked on the hardstands around the airfield perimeter, contemplating the fear and uncertainty and importance of the coming mission, their reverie was broken by a shout from Taylor in the nose. "Start engines!"

He had seen the flare that had been fired up from the center of the airfield silently signaling the engine start, and all over the airfield there arose a cacophony of noise with the whine of the inertia starters, then the coughing and popping of many engines coming to life. As much as possible, radio silence was maintained throughout the mission, but at engine start, every Englishman, farm animal, and secret German spy within hearing distance would know what was getting ready to happen.

This was a maximum effort mission, and the 303rd Bomb Group was putting up thirty-nine aircraft. The 358th Squadron was putting up nine, the 359th was sending ten, the 360th was sending eleven, and the 427th was putting up nine aircraft. Standard procedure was to start only the outermost engine on each wing to be used for the taxi out for takeoff, and soon the air was alive with the sound of seventy-eight engines totaling 97,500 horsepower, each engine producing 1250hp. The remaining engines would be started on each aircraft as it neared its takeoff position. The taxi to the active runway was long enough that it made sense to save fuel and wear on engines by only using two of them. After enough time had passed to get engines started and checked, another flare went up to signal that it was time to taxi to the runway. Slowly, in a manner planned, organized, and followed many times on previous missions, each aircraft entered the perimeter track circling the airfield and headed to the end of the active runway. Like a line of circus elephants walking head to tail, the bombers lumbered around the field, each starting the remaining engines at the designated location. They waited in line, moving up one position at a time, brakes squealing and groaning, as an aircraft took the runway and departed in a thunderous roar.

As each bomber inched its way to the runway, crewmen performed the last checks on the engines, made sure all the switches and indicators were in their proper positions, and stowed all loose items in their proper locations. The pilots knew to take the runway immediately after the bomber ahead of them had left the ground. Crewmen watched the tower for a flare indicating for them to hold their position, but with no flare, they automatically were cleared to go at the proper interval. While most of the attention was on the tower and the departing plane ahead, there was one sight that was inescapable…

…standing in the back of a jeep parked just off the end of the runway, where he would be visible by the crews of every bomber as they taxied into takeoff position, was Father Edmund Skoner, the Catholic chaplain. He was holding a Bible in one hand, the other up in the position of a last blessing. As in foxholes, there are no atheists in bombers heavy with explosives taking off into combat, so his efforts were welcomed by all who saw him. The fear was always there, but the real danger started at takeoff….

Shortly after 8:00 a.m., Jim Fowler taxied the *G.I. Sheets* into position on the runway, feeling the bomber being buffeted lightly by the propwash of the aircraft leaving ahead of it.

After getting the B-17 lined up on the runway, Barney Rawlings locked the tailwheel into its takeoff position, making the heavy aircraft easier to hold straight on takeoff until their speed became great enough for the big rudder on the tail to become effective. Fowler held the brakes as he pushed up all four throttles, unleashing 5,000 horsepower and a lot of noise. Rawlings reached over and put his left hand behind the throttles to make sure they didn't creep back and decrease the needed RPMs. As the bomber ahead of them began to lift off, Fowler called Ferguson in the tail gun position. "Any signal, Jack?"

Ferguson, who had a clear view of the tower, saw no red flare. "All clear, Skipper", was his reply.

Fowler announced, "Rolling. Start your clocks". Thompson and Dinwiddie made sure that their clock time for takeoff was noted in their logs for navigation and fuel burn calculations. The mission of the *G.I. Sheets* was starting. Fowler took his feet off of the brake pedals, and the aircraft jerked, then moved forward ponderously, but slowly accelerating. Again, an occasional buffet could be felt, the turbulence from the aircraft taking off ahead of them, but nothing to worry about. Fowler could feel the bomber getting lighter on its wheels, and took his right hand from the throttles and put it on the control yoke along with his left. Rawlings was still holding the throttles forward, and was watching the airspeed indicator, calling out speeds.

"Sixty! Eighty!", and then, "One hundred!"

At the one hundred mark, Fowler, eyes still down the runway ahead of him, trusted Rawlings' call and eased back the control yoke, coaxing the 68,000 lbs. of airplane into the air. Rawlings, still acting as Fowler's eyes on the instruments, said, "Positive climb!"

Fowler returned by saying, "Gear up!", and gave a thumbs up motion with his right hand, making sure that there was no mistake in the copilot's mind that he had ordered the landing gear to be raised. Rawlings reached over to the gear switch and lifted it. The sound of the gear could be heard as it retracted, and the aircraft smoothly accelerated after it was up and locked. At this point the crew could relax somewhat. For an aircraft loaded with bombs, there was no margin of error on takeoff. A blown tire, a misfiring engine or a distracted pilot could spell disaster.

Fowler flew straight ahead after takeoff to a predetermined altitude, then turned to the left to a northwesterly heading. They were flying deeper into England, not toward the target, and climbed steadily. On every bombing mission, there was an assembly plan that allowed the aircraft to join others in formation, and the process had to be followed to the letter, especially in reduced visibility. The more airplanes there were on a mission, the more complicated and dangerous the assembly process was. Many crews feared the assembly as much or more than the mission that followed. It was bad enough to have the enemy trying to kill you, but it was somehow more dreadful thinking that you might collide with one of your own aircraft in preparation to attacking the enemy.

The *G.I. Sheets* went into the clouds at about 1,000 feet, and Fowler climbed steadily on course using the directional instruments, keeping the proper heading. It was unspoken, but understood, that the hope was that the planes that had departed Molesworth ahead and above them were where they were supposed to be. Putting their faith in the planned assembly procedure, which was the only option, they continued to climb and topped out of the overcast just over 3,000 feet, finding themselves in clear air. At the proper time, they turned left toward a radio beacon that was being broadcast from Molesworth. As the big plane settled on the proper heading, still climbing, they sighted ahead of them the three bombers that were part of the element that they were to join. They kept up their speed, caught the three aircraft, and slipped into position as #4. Fowler eased the throttles back a bit to maintain position, and after flying just a short distance, Ferguson in the tail reported over the intercom that the number five and six aircraft had popped out of the clouds below and behind them and took their planned positions. Their small formation of six planes followed the planned procedure and started a climb to a higher altitude to join in with other groups of the bomber stream. As they climbed to the assigned altitude, the outside air temperature was decreasing, and the air became thinner. Rawlings got on the intercom and told the crew to don their oxygen masks and check them for proper flow. They were still below 10,000 feet, the altitude that required the oxygen masks to be used, but it was better to test them before you needed them. Standard procedure was for the crew members to check in to confirm that everything was working properly with the system. Problems with the oxygen system would be an automatic mission abort for a crew. Tragically, oxygen system problems were not uncommon, and there had been several deaths of crew members due to oxygen starvation.

All the crew members checked in over the intercom to confirm that they were breathing with no problems. The oxygen check also was a check on the intercom system as well. The intercom was another necessary item for a mission, also, if nothing else but for the gunners to tell the pilots of required evasive action because of attacking fighters. Everything seemed to be going according to plan as the aircraft climbed to their cruising altitude of 25,000 feet, slowly turning to the compass heading that would take them across the English Channel into France, on a path to Frankfurt. By this time, from the vantage point of *G.I. Sheets*, there was a seemingly endless line of bombers in front and behind them. The aircraft from various fields in England had formed into the long formation that would stretch for almost 400 miles.

When they knew that they were past the coast of England and headed over the English Channel, Fowler told the gunners to test their weapons. All gunner positions fired a short burst to assure that their guns were functioning properly. It was not unusual for a gun to have a belt feed problem or some other glitch. Better to find out over the Channel than in the heat of a fighter attack. With a mission to Frankfurt, in the heavily defended Ruhr Valley, there would definitely be fighter resistance.

As they were nearing the end of the climb to 25,000 feet, the two pilots noticed a problem. Each of the engines had a supercharger, a fan-like device that pumped extra air into the powerplant to allow it to develop more power. The actual benefit of the supercharger came into play at the higher altitudes where the engine needed the extra air to aid combustion. It was when they were climbing into the thinner air that the faulty supercharger made its presence known. It was apparent that the power of the number two engine (on the inboard side of the left wing) was not consistent with the power being produced by the other three engines. The higher they climbed, the less power it was producing. At 25,000 feet, number two was producing about half of its potential power. Obviously the supercharger had failed. They called Curt Finley down out of his flight position in the top gun turret and asked him to give them his opinion. Finley knew the B-17 inside and out, but there was nothing he could do. He concurred that the supercharger had failed, but as they suspected, nothing could be done in-flight to fix it. This was a job for the maintenance crews on the ground. They were headed into combat with three and one-half engines, not four. It was not the best situation, but how bad was it? Was it worthy of aborting the mission for the Fowler crew? Fowler and Rawlings found themselves having to make a decision, and quickly.

They had just crossed into German-held territory, and if they were going to abort the mission, they had to do it *now* so they could make the return back to the safety of England in a timely manner. If they continued and ended up having to turn around and head home while deep into German territory, the longer they would be without the protection of the guns of the other Fortresses in the formation. There were extra bombers in the formation to act as spares for exactly this kind of situation. All they had to do was turn around, and a spare would fly their slot. But the spares, if not needed, would be turning around to head home shortly. What should they do?

The two pilots decided to put it to the vote of the crew. When presented with the option of staying with the formation or returning to Molesworth, it was a quick vote. Everyone except Jack Ferguson wanted to stay on course to Frankfurt. Turning back home would leave them with one less mission toward the Magic Number 25, and besides, going back would make them look scared. And they wanted to be on this mission, the biggest of the war. And they had four engines, and only one of them was a little on the weak side. Everyone voted to press on, but there was one abstaining vote. Ferguson, the replacement gunner for the missing Harry Wallrobenstein, never felt that he was a true member of the crew. He felt that he was holding a place for the return of Wallrobenstein, and he didn't vote. He did say he was fine with whatever the rest wanted to do. They kept flying east toward Frankfurt planning on completing this mission, but the *G.I. Sheets* had other plans.

On a good day, with four good engines, a B-17G had to work hard just to keep up with the formation made up with B-17F models. Because of the ailing number two engine, the *G.I. Sheets* couldn't keep up the pace. Trying to keep up with the formation required that the three good engines had to be operated at higher power settings, which caused them to overheat, necessitating that they back off on the power. Reducing the power caused them to drift back in the formation. This situation continued all the way across France with drastic results. The Fowler crew found themselves lagging further and further back in the bomber stream, and they were soon too far into the mission to safely abort. And, of course, the spares had long ago left the formation for home, unneeded.

What was known by the pilots, but maybe not the crew, was that just two weeks before this mission there had been a bomber crew that had tried to abort very late in the mission. The result of that late abort had caused problems greater than simply one plane leaving the group.

The aircraft left the formation near the target, but had flown most of the mission with a mechanical problem. The ensuing abort caused other problems that could have been avoided had the pilot left formation at the earliest hint of trouble. The Eighth Air Force headquarters staff took note of this particular incident and issued a directive to all bomb wings under its command that *any* aircraft noting a problem that could impact the completion of the mission should abort at the earliest possible time. Fowler and Rawlings were aware of this order, but chose to pursue the completion of the mission to Frankfurt despite having an engine that was developing half its potential power.

Even more glaring was that the problem had become known barely past the English Channel, within a very short distance of Molesworth. Rather than exercise their command authority, they chose to let the crew vote on what to do.

I was able to communicate with Barney Rawlings several times prior to his passing, and had a chance to ask him about this decision to proceed on the mission rather than aborting it. He said that he felt that they all were blinded by their previous good luck. They had flown several missions with no problems whatsoever, and that perhaps they felt invincible. He did say, however, that he and Jim Fowler should have made a command decision to abort, and not put it to a vote of the crew. He also added that hindsight is rarely anything but perfect. And in playing the "what if" game, what if they had returned, only to face a worse mission the next day and were blown out of the sky by a direct flak burst or a Me-109?

So, they pressed on. Aside from the *G.I. Sheets* being plagued by its quirky out-of-rig control problems, things were otherwise all right. They were deep into France, but they were covered by a P-47 escort force that kept the German fighters away. The only problem was that they were slowly dropping back in the formation due to the lack of power on number two. They still had every intention of completing the mission successfully, even with the sick supercharger. The formation was long enough that even with their slower speed, they shouldn't run out of the tail end of the bomber string at their current speed. Joe Thompson had been giving Fowler reports of their estimated time to target, and the numbers looked good. In fact, they were just about to cross over into Germany, and the Initial Point for the bomb run into Frankfurt was getting close. Al Taylor would toggle his bombs when the planes around him dropped theirs, since their assigned element leader was now far ahead of them in the formation.

The closer to Germany they flew, the more heavily-defended the land below them would become. German fighters had not been a problem because of the P-47 escort, but flak would soon be trouble. Antiaircraft artillery, more commonly referred to as "triple-A" or "flak" was an insidious weapon. The Germans used several calibers of large guns to fire exploding shells upward toward the bombers flying overhead. The heavy steel shells weren't large (commonly the 88mm guns were used), but they were set to explode at whatever altitude the bombers were flying. The steel fragments of the shells would spread out from the point of the explosion, the hope being that bombers and crew members would be hit. When the flak gunners on the ground had a good fix on the altitude of the bombers, the sky would be peppered with small black puffs of the rapidly firing guns. The flak bursts looked so benign, like small balls of black wool, but they were deadly. Steel fragments could easily puncture the thin skin of a B-17, ripping out oxygen lines, control cables, and electrical wiring. They could also rip through a crewman's flight suit and into his body like a large caliber bullet. Those that could wore or sat on flak vests for protection, but the thing about flak was that you never knew where it would come from or where it might penetrate the plane or your body. To make it worse, there was absolutely no defense for it other than the flak vest and steel helmet that most wore. You just hoped it wasn't your day to be a victim.

Since finding the sick supercharger on the number two engine just after crossing the Channel, everyone's attention was on that engine. Like a doctor checking the pulse on a critically ill patient, the pilots and engineer Finley kept checking the instruments and kept glancing at it periodically as if they could see into its metallic heart. Since their attention was naturally focused on number two, not long after getting into the flak fields, the plane was pummeled by a nearby WHOOMPH, and they were buffeted by the blast. The *G.I. Sheets* was peppered by flak fragments, and Fowler asked over the intercom about damage. A couple of the guys said that they'd been slightly wounded, but nothing serious. However, Curt Finley, in the top turret, saw that engine number four on the right wing was in trouble.

"Top turret to pilot. Number four is losing oil, skipper! Bad!"

Unlike the supercharger, which just reduced the power when it failed, losing engine oil could be disastrous on many levels. The oil was there to lubricate and help cool the engine. As the pilots looked at the engine and saw the oil streaming out, they could tell from the amount that it was soon going to lose it all.

When it did, the engine would seize up if it didn't outright self-destruct and fall off the wing or catch fire. It had to be shut down immediately. To complicate matters, the propeller had to be "feathered", or streamlined in order to reduce drag and keep the engine from turning after it was shut down. The feathering system was driven by oil pressure, so it all had to be done immediately if there was hope of avoiding disaster. Fowler and Rawlings went through the shutdown and feathering procedures just as they had trained and practiced for numerous times. Thankfully, there was enough oil left in the engine to feather the stopped propeller blades.

The *G.I. Sheets* now had one good engine on the right wing, and one and one-half engines on the left wing. It could no longer hold its position in the formation, and it was actually now an impediment to the other aircraft, just like the bomber that had left the formation a few weeks prior, resulting in the abort directive sent out by Eighth Air Force Headquarters.

Geographically, the *G.I. Sheets* was very near the Initial Point when they lost the number four engine. They were actually only about ten minutes from the target, but continuing to the release point was no longer an option. They were close enough, however, that they could see some bombers a few miles ahead starting a left turn, beginning the egress from the target and starting the trip back to England after dropping their bombs. The best course of action, Fowler knew, was to try to intersect the returning stream of bombers and seek protection in their numbers. German fighters were always on the lookout for crippled stragglers, and wouldn't pass up the chance for an easy kill. Fowler immediately turned out of the formation and toward the bombers headed back home. He called on the intercom to inform the crew, and to tell Taylor to unload the bombs to save the weight and to get the high explosives out of their plane. Shortly everyone could tell the bomb bay doors were opening, and as Taylor dropped all of the bombs, they felt the plane lurch upward, suddenly lighter by 6,000 lbs.

Getting back into the bomber stream was a good idea, but the distance was too great. As soon as they left the inbound bomber stream and set out for the safety of the returning formation, Finley, in the top turret, spotted a group of four Me-109s high over them, flying parallel to their course. He called out over the intercom, warning the pilots and gunners, hoping to give them time to prepare for the attack that was sure to come now that they were a straggler, out of the formation and its protection.

The Messerschmitts flew out ahead of them, falling into a line trailing one another, then made a 180 degree turn to reverse course in order to attack the B-17 head on. This was a tactic that the Luftwaffe pilots often chose because the nose of the B-17 was the most vulnerable point, and the head on attack was quick because of the high closing speed as the fighters and the bomber approached each other.

As the fighters dove quickly down on them, there was nothing that the Fowler crew could do but face the attack, and try to use the top turret .50 caliber machine guns and those in the G-model's chin turret, the cursed contraption that had slowed them down. As the Messerschmitts came into range, Fowler and Rawlings kicked the B-17 around in as much of a defensive maneuver as the bulky bomber could manage. Finley fired his guns in the top turret, but before the chin turret ever fired a shot, there was a series of loud bangs and the acrid smell of gun powder was evident in the plane. The 20mm cannon on one of the attacking fighters had scored hits on the nose of the bomber. As the planes flew past, the guns in the rear of the *G.I. Sheets* started firing at the passing fighters, the gunners trying the best they could, but only the tail gun and the ball turret had an unrestricted fields of fire. The Me-109s were diving too fast and were too far below Ferguson for him to get off an effective shot, but he tried to no avail. It was odd that Arrington in the ball turret hadn't fired a shot. Unbeknownst to anyone at this point, Arrington's turret was inoperative. His parachute, hanging on a hook above the turret in the fuselage (the ball was too cramped for him to wear the parachute) had become dislodged during the violent evasive action of the bomber, and had fallen on top of the ball, jamming the gear system that rotated it. Luckily, the ball had jammed in a position that allowed the exit hatch to open into the fuselage, and Arrington was able to escape the turret and avoid a potential disaster. The only problem: his parachute was chewed into an unusable mess by the ball's gears. If the order came to bail out of the stricken bomber, he would be unable to jump. Arrington had tried to call out over the intercom to the rest of the crew to tell them of his predicament, but received no answer. Either the intercom wasn't working, or nobody had time to answer him in the heat of the attack by the Messerschmitts.

There was a strong wind blowing through the B-17 that hadn't been there before the attack by the fighters. It was evident that the nose of the bomber had been shattered, and the cold gale was howling through the plane from the navigator/bombardier compartment. Fowler called over the intercom, but all he heard in response was static.

Compounding the problem, the pilots were finding that it was a struggle to breathe, which meant that the oxygen system had been damaged or destroyed. Fowler put the bomber in a tight, diving turn, trying to get to a lower altitude and breathable air, and hopefully away from the German fighters. During the spiraling dive, Rawlings caught sight of the Messerschmitts. They were departing, heading for another lone B-17 straggler. A couple of more turns in the dive, and the other B-17 could be seen spinning down, trailing smoke, and the Messerschmitts were heading back toward *G.I. Sheets*, obviously intending to finish it off. It was discovered later that this other B-17 that was shot down by the attacking Me-109s was seen going down in flames and was mistakenly reported later as being Fowler's plane.

The smoking B-17 that the Messerschmitt's had shot down had disappeared into a cloud deck below them. That gave Fowler an escape plan. He forced the nose down further, headed for the clouds. Better to risk blowing the wings off the bomber than facing certain demise at the guns of the Me-109s. Rawlings caught a glance at the airspeed indicator, and the needle was registering over 300 mph and rising fast…and the never-exceed speed was 270 mph. During the crash dive to the clouds, he had the thought that maybe he should tell the crew what was going on, sure that they must be thinking that they were in an uncontrolled descent toward their deaths. When he tried the intercom, all he got in response was mostly clicks and pops, but did hear a garbled word or two. He hoped that they heard enough to know that the plane, though shot up, was under some semblance of control, and that they shouldn't try to bail out…not yet, anyway.

Finally, after a long, screaming dive for over 18,000 feet, the *G.I. Sheets* reached the cloud deck they had been seeking. Rawlings had no idea how fast they were going on the way down…he was afraid to look at the airspeed indicator. But they were now hidden in the clouds at 5,000 feet. At that point, besides the oxygen system and the intercom, they discovered that apparently there had been damage to some of the flight instruments that allowed them to fly in zero visibility. The concept of "flying blind" is difficult for non-pilots to grasp. Without seeing the ground or a definite horizon, and lacking the proper instrumentation and training, it is impossible to fly an airplane in controlled flight. Without the proper visual cues, spatial disorientation and vertigo occur and the pilot simply loses control of the aircraft. The pilots had plenty of instruction on how to fly "blind", but to do so, the instruments had to be operating properly.

Luck held out for the Fowler crew in that the basic instrumentation had survived the attack, and the aircraft could be controlled well enough to remain safely in the clouds in order to hide from the German fighters. But how long could they stay in the clouds?

Again, they found themselves with no choice. They would stay in the clouds as long as they could. They simply held a westerly heading, pointing generally toward England, and definitely away from German-occupied territory.

After getting the aircraft into the clouds and stabilized, the pilots discovered that the rudimentary autopilot that was used mostly for the bomb run from the Initial Point to the target, could be used to help hold the airplane on course, allowing the pilots the chance to take stock of the damage to plane and crew, and how to best handle the situation that they were in.

Rawlings peered out his right window at the dead number four engine, and was shocked at what he saw. When he had last looked at the engine, before the fighter attack and the screaming dive to safety, the propeller had been feathered in order to streamline it, reducing drag and keeping the engine from seizing from lack of oil, possibly ripping the engine from the wing.

He blinked, not believing his eyes. There was *no* propeller on number four! Apparently, at some point in the high-speed dive from 23,000 feet to the clouds below, the propeller had become unfeathered, allowing it to rotate again. For whatever mechanical reason, the propeller had separated from the engine, leaving the aircraft. When a propeller on a multi-engine aircraft fails catastrophically, most of the time there is major damage due to the blades striking the fuselage or wing. Neither pilot saw, heard, or felt the blades leaving the engine, and there was apparently no damage to the plane when the separation occurred. Finley, in his vantage point in the top turret, was also oblivious to anything happening to the propeller. Even more amazing, the spinning blades didn't cause the oil-dry engine to seize and break from its mounts, taking a large portion of the wing with it. In the midst of the terror of the attack, a miracle had been bestowed on *G.I. Sheets*, the three blades of the propeller flung off into space, and not one touching the aircraft.

After the bomber was safely in the clouds and stabilized, the autopilot allowed the aircraft to be handled by one pilot. Because of the recalcitrant intercom, Finley was sent back into the aft portion of the bomber to check the status of Dinwiddie and the gunners. Rawlings left the cockpit to check the damage to the nose compartment.

Finley found that all of the crewmen (including himself) in the rear of the plane were doing satisfactorily, but all had experienced flak wounds to varying degrees. None of the wounds were life-threatening, but they were wounds just the same. A flak round had apparently exploded under the bomber, sending fragments up through the lower fuselage. Dinwiddie was peppered with small wounds in his back and the backs of his legs. The gunners also were mostly hit in the lower extremities. Nobody had any head wounds nor had been hit by large fragments.

Rawlings didn't find things as encouraging in the nose. After making his way down into the nose, he found it a shambles. Both crewmen had been seriously wounded. Taylor had taken a 20mm round through his upper leg, and Thompson had a very bloody scalp wound. Both men had metal and plexiglass fragments embedded in their exposed flesh. Thompson had fragments in his eyes. Rawlings was surprised to see that the men had been able to bandage each other's wounds with the first aid kit in the nose compartment. Both were in severe pain, but had not injected any morphine for fear of falling asleep. They wanted to be awake in case they had to abandon the aircraft. The frigid wind blowing through the destroyed nose did little to improve their situation, but there was nothing to be done about it. They were unable to climb through the small hatch into the main fuselage because of their wounds. Rawlings made his way back to the cockpit, leaving the two seriously wounded men in the frigid compartment.

As it sometimes happens in the middle of traumatic and frightening circumstances, humor shines through. Rawlings related a strange and humorous thing that happened just after he returned from checking on

Thompson and Taylor. After they had been in the clouds for a few minutes, headed westward, there had been periods of the clouds becoming thin in places. An occasional German fighter could be seen here and there, obviously searching for the escaped bomber. The clouds hampered the enemy pilots as much as it did the Americans. There was no airborne search radar in the typical fighter planes at that time, so it was a matter of actually putting eyeballs on your target. Everyone was hindered by the low visibility.

After Rawlings returned from the nose and got strapped back in his seat, Jim Fowler left his position to go aft to look at the intercom wiring, leaving Rawlings to watch the instruments and mind the progress of the plane. As Jim left his seat, Barney was looking out the windshield just as they passed through a hole in the clouds.

To his surprise, slightly ahead and above their left wing was a Focke Wulf FW-190, just as if they were purposely flying very close formation with each other. Apparently the German fighter pilot was searching for them, but when they both flew through the hole, the enemy pilot was looking in the opposite direction. Rawlings said he would forever have the image of that pilot etched in his mind…the German pilot was a blond young man, his helmet and goggles loose and pushed back on his head. He was looking up and down on the side away from the bomber, and when he turned his head to the right and saw the B-17 flying along side him, his eyes went wide. He immediately rolled his fighter away to the left, diving away from them, never returning. Barney said that the surreal experience was over in seconds. Like the miracle of the lost propeller, it was a matter of good fortune that the two enemies joined up with each other in the clouds without colliding. Formation flying is difficult enough when you can see each other, and the two aircraft joining up, perfectly matching speeds and direction while flying blind in the clouds was beyond believable.

As near as could be calculated, the *G.I. Sheets* had been flying in and out of the clouds for slightly over an hour, after leaving the formation just short of Frankfurt. Fowler had no idea where they were, but he and Rawlings estimated that they were probably over Belgium, and a good distance from Germany. Although the Belgians were our allies, the country was occupied by the Germans. Being over Belgium

Fowler Crew, Dyersburg Field, Dyersburg, Tennessee, Fall 1943. Photo taken near the completion of Advanced B-17 Combat Training. Back Row, l-r: Jim Fowler, Bernard Rawlings, Alvin Taylor, Joe Thompson. Front Row, l-r: Curtis Finley, Richard Arrington, Don Dinwiddie, Loren Zimmer, Miller Jackson, Harry Wallrobenstein.

Fowler Crew, RAF Molesworth, December 4, 1943, photo taken while undergoing orientation with 303rd Bomb Group, 427th Squadron. Back Row, l-r: Jim Fowler, Bernard Rawlings, Joe Thompson, Al Taylor. Front Row, l-r: Curtis Finley, Richard Arrington, Don Dinwiddie, Loren Zimmer, Harry Wallrobenstein, Miller Jackson.

Aerial photo of RAF Molesworth. Circular areas around the perimeter of the field are hardstands where bombers were parked.

RAF Molesworth. Ground staff awaiting the return of bombers from a mission.

Hell's Angels, a B-17F of the 303rd Bomb Group. The crew is sitting on top of plane, with ground crew on stand, and armorers on the bomb. Note the plexiglass bombardier compartment. Each of the bombs painted on the nose represent a mission successfully flown by this plane, not by this particular crew.

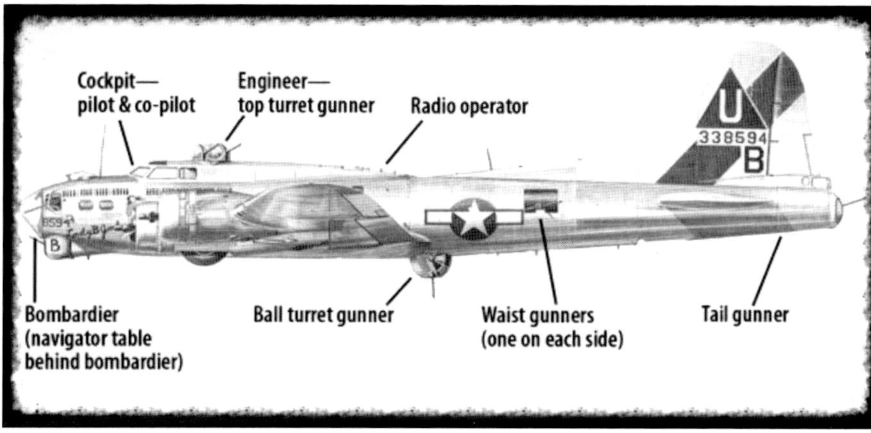

Crew position locations in a typical B-17.

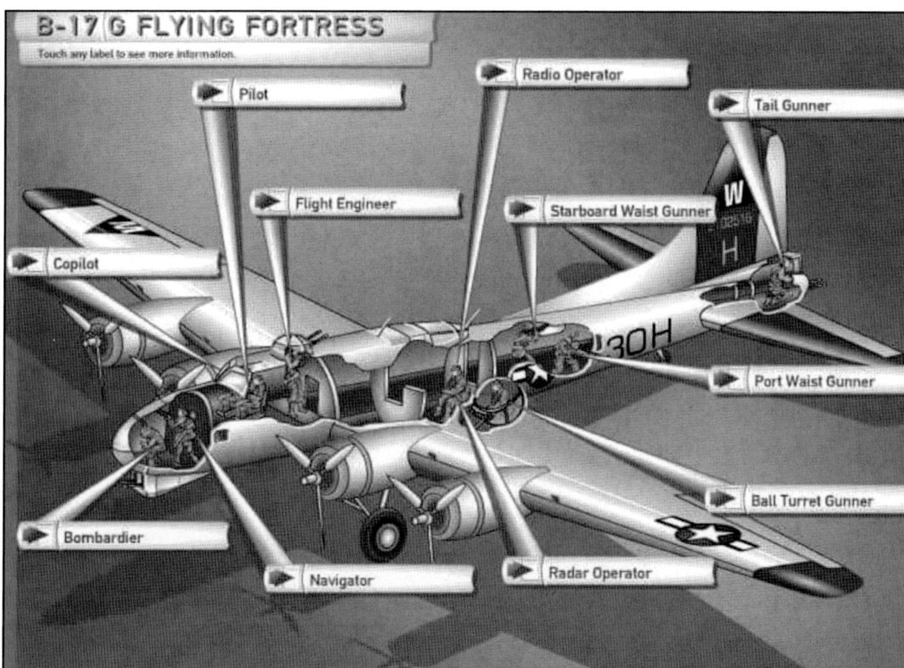

Another drawing of crew positions. Note that "Radio Operator" is also listed as "Radar Operator". Radar was in later models, not typically used in most of the bombing campaign until near war's end.

Nose of B-17G showing cheek guns, chin turret, top turret, and bombardier's station in the nose.

View of pilots' station of typical B-17. Pilot's flight controls are on the left, co-pilot's on the right. The engine controls are in the center, shared by both pilots.

The only known photo of the G.I. Sheets *other than the one in the field after it had crashed. This photo was taken at some point during maintenance. The name was only partially painted on the nose, and the cowling for the chin turret machine guns had been removed and the guns were not present.*

Capt. Bob Sheets, the pilot for whom the G.I. Sheets *was named by his crew.*

B-17s taxiing out for takeoff. Note: the inboard engines are shut off to conserve fuel.

Bombs and ammunition being loaded into a B-17 of 303rd Bomb Group. This is a 5,000 lb bomb load comprised of ten 500 lb bombs. The boxes to the right of photo are belts of .50 cal ammo for machine guns.

Artist's rendition of a navigator (foreground) and bombardier in B-17. Note the "cheek" guns mounted on the left and right sides and the spent shell casings. The nose of the B-17 was very vulnerable to fighter attacks. German pilots would frequently choose a frontal attack on any bomber that was alone and not in formation with other bombers.

Top secret Norden bombsight that enabled American bombers to accurately hit targets from several thousand feet.

Vaults where Norden bombsights were stored and guarded.

Waist gunners on B-17. Close quarters and wind coming through gun ports made this an uncomfortable position to man. LIFE *magazine photo*

Waist gunner wearing a flak vest. The vests added to the discomfort of standing at this gun position. Note the shell casings on the floor that made it difficult to move without slipping.

Top turret on B-17 with two .50 caliber Browning machine guns. The turret was electrically powered and could rotate 360 degrees.

Above: *Sperry ball turret on the belly of a B-17. The ball could travel in a 360 degree circle and the guns traversed up and down.*

Right: *Artist's rendition of the seating position of ball turret gunner. This was a job for a gunner who was not claustrophobic.*

Tailgunner's position on B-17. The gunner would crawl through the aft portion of the fuselage to reach his position.

Only photo found of tail gunner Jack Ferguson (front row, 4th from left), with his originally assigned crew (Ness) before transfer to the Fowler crew as a replacement for the missing Harry Wallrobenstein.

Partial view of radio operator's compartment.

Radio operator's compartment in another B-17. This photo shows a more complete position, with flight instruments on the left wall and the radio on the back of the desk. Note the bailout bell on the wall above the radio. Having heat was a luxury that the radio operator could enjoy.

Don Dinwiddie at the radio operator's station in a B-17 on display at a Cape Girardeau, Missouri airshow, circa 1991. This was the first time he had been in a B-17 since the mission on January 29, 1944.

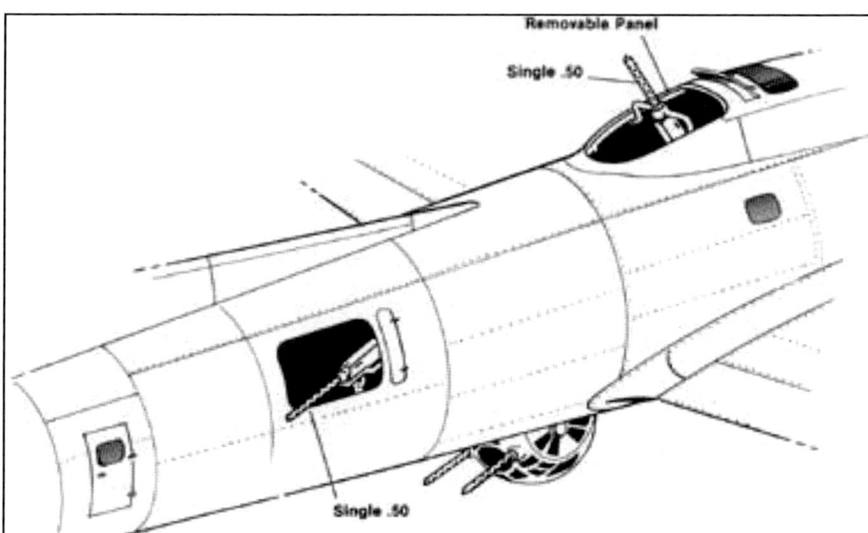

Drawing showing the radio operator's gun (top of fuselage, firing rearward only).

Two versions of the 303rd Bomb Group patch.

Birds of the 303rd Bomb Group featured the triangle "C" tail markings, shown on this B-17G of the 359th Bomb Squadron.

Boeing B-17G nose detail. U.S. Air Force photo

B-17 G formation bomb drop, ca. 1944. U.S. Air Force photo

B-17 formation flying through antiaircraft (flak) bursts. View is from the right waist gunner's position.

Shoulder patch of the 427th Squadron. There were several iterations of the Bugs Bunny patch, but all of them showed him standing with one foot on a bomb. Some showed the famous "What's up, Doc?" quote, and some had him wearing a blue heated flying suit—the "bunny suit"—as it was nicknamed by the flight crews.

B-17F formation over Schweinfurt, Germany, August 17, 1943.

Flak damage to left wing of B-17.

P-51 Mustang often used as an escort for the bombers. Note the drop tanks under the wings.

Redtail P-51's of the Tuskegee Airmen escorting a B-17. The African-American fighter pilots were very aggressive, never losing a bomber on any of their escort missions. Don recollected being escorted by them.

British Spitfires often escorted U.S. bombers on shorter missions because it did not have the fuel capacity for the longer missions into Germany.

P-38 Lightning was nicknamed "The Fork-Tailed Devil" by the Germans. They truly feared the Lightning when it escorted the bomber formations. The black and white stripes were painted on all aircraft used during the D-Day invasion on June 6, 1944 in order to quickly identify them, hence the name "invasion stripes" that is often a referral to the paint scheme.

The P-47 Thunderbolt was a workhorse, used as an escort fighter and ground attack aircraft. It was nick-named "The Jug" because of its shape. It appears large and bulky but was very maneuverable and was able to sustain major battle damage and keep flying.

The DeHavilland Mosquito used by the British in multiple roles. It was the fastest piston-engined aircraft of the war and was excellent for fast reconnaissance and pinpoint bombing missions for difficult targets.

Messerschmitt Me-109, similar to the four aircraft that attacked the G.I. Sheets *after it dropped out of formation near Frankfurt, just short of the target.*

Focke Wulf FW-190s from the Jg-26 detachment at Florennes Luftwaffe Field in Belgium. These aircraft are similar to the two aircraft that forced the G.I. Sheets *to land near Solre Saint Gery, Belgium.*

Site of the crash landing of the G.I. Sheets *in Marly's Field, Solre Saint Gery, Belgium. The villagers attempted to burn the aircraft to prevent the Germans from looting it, but failed to totally destroy it. Note the barrels and fuel pump on the wing, evidence that the Germans were trying to drain the fuel for use in their own aircraft. Even in early 1944, the Germans were experiencing a fuel shortages due to the Allied bombing of their refineries and fuel transportation facilities. The field was muddy and relatively short for landing such a large aircraft, but with the wheels retracted, it slid to a stop in a short distance. Note the missing propeller on the #4 engine (far left side of photo) that came off during the high-speed dive toward the clouds in an attempt to evade the attacking Messerschmitt Me-109s near Frankfurt.*

Oberleutnant Wolfgang Neu, (both photos above) commander of the Jg-26 Fighter Unit at Florennes, Belgium. He and fellow pilot Oberleutnant Kurt Kranefeld gave chase to the G.I. Sheets *after it flew over their field. They fired on the B-17, wounding Miller Jackson and Jack Ferguson. They ceased firing when they saw that the plane was attempting to land. Neu, who shot down twelve Allied aircraft, was killed in April 1944 by an American P-47. Kranefeld was killed two months later.*

Twenty-four year old Andree de Jongh, the Belgian woman who developed the escape plan known as the "Comet Line". This clandestine operation was able to aid over 800 downed Allied aviators in evading capture and return to England. Her code name with Allied intelligence was "The Postwoman".

Dr. Maurice Verstraeten, leader of the Comet Line in the Solre Saint Gery area. He was nicknamed "Dr. Moto" by the downed aviators because of the motor scooter he rode in visiting his patients. Because he was a physician, the Germans allowed him to use the scooter and gave him a gasoline ration in order to make his medical rounds, not suspecting that he was also using it to visit the downed airmen that he was aiding.

Georges Vandeput, Denise Siquiet, and Arthur Derenne in 1987. Arthur was a 14-year-old boy in 1944 who aided the Fowler crew after the crash. All three were instrumental in building the monument to the crew.

Sylvie Derenne, Dr. Verstraeten, and Anne Dorignaux in 1987. Sylvie was an active member of the underground in 1944 and instrumental in hiding and aiding the Fowler crew. Anne helped organize the monument dedication in 1987 and acted as the author's interpreter in his visit to Belgium in 1988.

Rene' Bouvigne, who was a member of the underground while in his teens. He acted as a courier and delivered messages during his commute to college. He never knew who his contacts were but would leave and pick up messages from secret hiding places. He found out after the war that his contacts were two of his college professors. His widowed mother and his 10-year-old sister were also active in the underground.

Jim Fowler, Maurice Lamendin, and Don Dinwiddie, 1987. Lamendin was very active in the underground, and hid Jim and Don in his barn after the crash on January 29, 1944. He and Dr. Verstraeten then moved the two airmen several miles north of Solre Saint Gery to the home of his grandmother, where they stayed for most of their time while in hiding in Belgium.

Ball turret gunner Richard Arrington wearing civilian clothing while in hiding after the crash in Belgium. Arrington and navigator Joe Thompson, stayed together on a local farm until they were liberated in September of 1944.

Copilot Barney Rawlings (right), Dale Kinert (left, an evading B-24 navigator), and a young French boy. The two airmen were staying with the boy's family as they were making their trek across France to Spain.

Gunner Loren Zimmer (right) with downed British pilot John Leyne while hiding at the home of Maurice Lamendin, circa 1944. Leyne had bailed out of his Halifax bomber over Belgium on a night bombing mission and was moved into the Solre Saint Gery area by the underground.

Loren Zimmer (left) with farmer Albert Rolin in 1987. Zimmer had bailed out of the crippled G.I. Sheets *at an altitude too low for his chute to fully open, and luckily landed uninjured in a swampy bog on Rolin's farm. He was rescued and hidden by Rolin after the incident.*

House where Don and Jim hid for most of their time in Belgium. They were taken to this house in La Malaise, near Thirimont. The house was the home of Hermance Miot, grandmother of Maurice Lamendin. Photo circa 1987.

Madame Hermance Miot

wasn't as good as being over England, but it was better than being over Germany.

If they had to bail out over Belgium there was a chance to be helped by the Belgians, not beaten to death by the German civilians, which unfortunately, had been the fate of some Allied bomber crews who had been forced down over Germany. By this point in the war, it was common knowledge that if you had to bail out over Germany, you'd better hope to be captured by German military and not civilians. The military men would capture you and you'd end up in a POW camp, but the civilians would probably kill you. After all, you were the guys who had been dropping bombs on them for the past year. Capture was the best of the possibilities that awaited you after you hit German soil.

The bomber had made relatively good progress since leaving the formation near the target, especially considering that it had only one good engine on the right side, and one and a half on the left side. The head on attack on by the Messerschmitts had been devastating, but it could have been much worse. Thompson and Taylor had serious wounds, but they were still alive. The nose of the bomber had suffered substantial damage, but it was still flying. The clouds had been a perfect hiding place for their flight back toward England. Without them, the *G.I. Sheets* would have been shot down. A lone B-17 was no match for even a single Luftwaffe fighter, and the Germans seldom attacked a bomber with one fighter.

Suddenly, the clouds ceased to exist. The bomber broke out of the edge of the cloud cover into the bright sky. Immediately, the gunners in the rear saw that they had just overflown a German airfield. Arrington, who had no gun now that his turret was out of commission, and not trusting the faulty intercom, immediately went forward to the cockpit to deliver the bad news to Fowler and Rawlings. By the time that he had returned to the rear of the plane, the bad news had just gotten much worse. The airfield was apparently home to a fighter squadron, because two Focke Wulf FW-190s had just taken off and were rapidly climbing toward the crippled bomber.

Oberleutnant Wolfgang Neu and his wingman, Oberleutnant Kurt Kranefeld had just finished getting fuel and a fresh load of ammo after a busy morning. The huge Allied raid to Frankfurt had resulted in every German fighter available to be ready to attack the bombers to and from the target. The Allies had employed dozens of escort fighters to protect the formations, and the Germans hadn't done well against them. Not that anyone would admit it in the High Command, but the lack of fuel and a Luftwaffe staffed by young poorly-trained pilots were not a match for the American P-51s, P-47s, and the P-38s.

Trying to attack a large formation of B-17s protected by such aircraft and pilots was ineffective and suicidal. But just as the ground crews finished preparing their aircraft for another sortie, a target dropped in their lap. The sound came first…the deep throb of several engines, and as their eyes swept the sky, a lone B-17 appeared out of the clouds just a few thousand feet above them, headed west, alone. Neu, who had stepped away from the aircraft for a smoke while the ground crews tended to their duties, rapidly threw the cigarette down, ground it out with his boot, and yelled at Kranefeld to get ready to go. This was the kind of easy target that they wished for…a lone bomber. The two pilots quickly climbed into their cockpits, got strapped in, and started their engines.

From his vantage point in the rear of the bomber, Jack Ferguson saw the two Focke Wulfe fighters quickly climbing toward them. He didn't bother with trying the intercom, but he knew that the sound of his guns would let the pilots know what he was doing. He opened fire on the fighters when they came into range. Unfortunately, his attempt at defending the B-17 was like spitting in the face of a hungry lion. Both of the German fighters returned fire, raking the rear section of the bomber with 20mm shells as they overtook it.

As the fighters pulled up and away in order to come around for another attack, Fowler tried to kick the *G.I. Sheets* around to give the gunners a better opportunity at firing on them. He found the rudder unresponsive, the control cables obviously damaged in the attack. To make matters much worse, the number three engine on the right wing was trailing oil, and the propeller blades slowing down. He ordered Rawlings to shut down the engine and to try to feather the prop. There was no doubt that the *G.I. Sheets* was coming down, and the problem was where. The only power was coming from engine number one on the left wing, with some help from the anemic number two. With the control cables to the rudder damaged, there was not much to do but go straight ahead with no possibility of turning the descending aircraft. With two dead engines on the right wing, the aircraft was almost uncontrollable. If Fowler let the airspeed drop too low, the aircraft would roll over and go into the ground. And to make matters worse, the FW-190s were coming back around for another pass.

As if by a miracle, Fowler saw a muddy farm field directly ahead of the descending bomber. It was their only hope of survival. They were too low to bail out, and even if they were at a higher altitude, he thought of Arrington's plight of not having a parachute. He lowered the landing gear of the stricken B-17. Thankfully, the German pilots saw the gear coming down and realized that the bomber was finished. Lowering the gear was the universal sign that the aircraft was intending to land.

Neu took a position off the left wing of the bomber, and his wingman Kranefeld took a position above and behind it, ready to fire on the plane if the bomber crew attempted to shoot at them. The lack of defensive fire from the bomber was ominous.

It was either a trap, or the gunners were incapacitated, or the pilots knew there was no chance of staying in the air and were giving up the fight. At any rate, the German pilots stood off, stopping their attack on the bomber.

Rawlings yelled at Finley to go back to the rear compartment to spread the word that they were going to be making a forced landing. He made it through the bomb bay to Dinwiddie's radio compartment, and asked him to relay the warning to the gunners that the bailout bell would ring just before hitting the ground so they could brace for impact.

The field where they intended to land appeared very muddy. Fowler ordered Rawlings to retract the gear. The landing gear would only get trapped in the mud on impact and result in the bomber flipping onto its back. A belly landing was the only safe option. Fowler had to judge his descent carefully, because there was a line of trees at the approach end of the field. He saw a gap in the trees that he hoped the B-17s wide wings would fit between. At the other end of the field there appeared to be a small village. At least, he thought, maybe some people might come help them out of the wrecked airplane if he messed up the landing. The altimeter read about 400 feet above the ground when Fowler had Rawlings ring the bailout bell so that the crew could brace for the impending impact with the muddy field. All of the crew members who were able to comply got into positions against the fuselage bulkheads near the radio compartment. As the airplane slid over the tree line, Rawlings killed the remaining two engines to reduce the possibility of fire. Fowler held the B-17 off as long as possible, slowing it down, but the big plane hit the ground roughly and finally slid to a stop in the wet farm field.

When the bomber finally stopped moving, everyone exited the plane as quickly as possible. The situation was chaotic; the fear and adrenaline of the crash, the German fighters, and the whole crazy morning of bad engines and the failure to complete the mission had taken their toll on the crew. Plus, it was now evident, most of them were wounded. As often happens when enduring traumatic experiences, memories fail or become confused. The crew members later tried to recollect what happened, with various differences.

Barney Rawlings was the only crew member that later wrote his recollections. Don Dinwiddie, my father-in-law, verbally spoke of his memories of the crash.

The crash site was immediately visited by local villagers who had witnessed the crash landing, and their memories were also revisited in later years.

After seventy-six years, a more complete picture of what really happened can finally be pieced together. For the rest of this chapter, only the events that happened and were witnessed by most of the crew will be examined. In the following chapter, the reality of what *did* happen will be discussed.

According to Barney Rawlings, when the plane stopped sliding over the rough and muddy field, everyone wasted no time in leaving the aircraft. He climbed out through the right side window near his copilot's position. He had no idea how Jim Fowler exited the plane. Rawlings said his first thought was getting Thompson and Taylor out of their nose compartment, but was surprised to find both of them lying on the ground ahead of the nose of the aircraft. Jim Fowler was checking on their condition. They had apparently been thrown through the broken plexiglass nose when the aircraft suddenly stopped.

Don Dinwiddie and Richard Arrington were carrying Miller Jackson from the plane, and Curt Finley was trying to get to Jack Ferguson in the tail. Both Jackson and Ferguson had serious wounds, from a combination of the flak over the target area, and the cannon fire from the German fighter aircraft.

As the more able crew members were moving the wounded away from the crashed plane, two young boys came running up to them. The oldest appeared to be perhaps in his late teens, the younger around ten or twelve. They were excitedly trying to talk to Rawlings and Fowler, but they were speaking French. Rawlings had a high school knowledge of French, and tried to speak to the boys, but it wasn't working out well. Rawlings' first concern was finding out the geographical location of where they had landed. The older of the two boys finally pointed to the ground and said, "Belgique!" Rawlings was relieved.

Although logic told him that after flying west though the clouds for almost two hours, they wouldn't be in Germany, but he was relieved to have that fact reinforced. The last place that he wanted to be was in the country that they were trying to bomb.

As they were all standing there in a state of disbelief of what was happening, the roar of an airplane engine became apparent. One of the Focke Wulf fighters was circling high overhead, but the other was diving down on them.

From all appearances, the diving FW-190 was preparing to strafe them, but nobody reacted by running or hiding. They all stood there stupidly staring at the sight of the blunt-nosed fighter bearing down on them.

Oberleutnant Neu was mystified that the men on the ground were just standing there, staring at his approach. But Neu also knew of the strange things a man would do during the horror of war, and he could feel some of what these men were feeling. He had seen many of his friends killed and wounded in this war. All he had to do was squeeze the trigger on his control stick and spray these frozen men with cannon shells, but he felt that he had done his part for the Fatherland and had put this Fortress and its crew out of action. He was not a fanatic like the crazy Hitler, thinking that they could actually win this war. The war was over for these boys on the ground, just as one day his would be over. He dove toward them at over 350mph, roared over them at treetop height, then pulled up into a climbing victory roll, and went to join Kranefeld. They would go back to their base at Florennes, report the crash of the bomber and its location, and he would be done with this part of his war. Tomorrow it would begin again, with a sky full of Allied bombers and fighters coming to destroy his country, and he would do his best to stop them. If he didn't get shot down by a P-38 or P-47, maybe he'd do something to get a medal pinned on him by some fat desk-bound colonel, ostensibly for "defending the Reich."

To Barney Rawlings, time seemed to have become elastic…speeding up, slowing down. It all seemed dream-like to him, and nothing made sense. More people from the village showed up; one was a man in a clerical collar, obviously a priest, and one a man who was trying to ride a motor scooter over the muddy field.

Rawlings and Finley went to where Dinwiddie and Arrington were kneeling over Miller Jackson. Jackson had a terrible abdominal wound, and was bleeding profusely. The man on the motor scooter pushed his way through the men to Jackson. He had a small bag, and was obviously a doctor. As the doctor tended to Jackson, Ferguson asked for a cigarette. Someone found one and lit it for him, and Jackson then asked for one, too. The doctor backed away from Jackson, indicating to his crew mates that they should give him a cigarette. It was apparent from the doctor's demeanor that Jackson was near death. Finley gave Jackson a cigarette, and then backed away and was standing by Rawlings as the doctor went to check on Thompson and Taylor.

Rawlings said later that seeing Miller Jackson soaked in his own blood was the first time that he realized that he was *really* in a war. In another surrealistic moment, Rawlings then looked up at the top turret on the crashed bomber, saw Finley's helmet draped over the rear of one of the machine guns, and felt panic flow through his mind. He yelled, "We have to get Finley out of there! He's trapped!" As he was yelling, he was grabbing the arm of Curt Finley, who was standing next to him. Finley assured him that he was alright.

The doctor indicated that Thompson, Taylor, Ferguson, and Jackson needed to be moved out of the field to the nearby road in order to be transported to the closest hospital. While some of the local men helped with that, the oldest of the two young boys pantomimed to Rawlings and Finley that they should leave the area lest the Germans come capture them. He pointed to a vehicle coming their way on a distant road.

Rawlings and Finley looked around. Don Dinwiddie and Jim Fowler were gone, and so was Arrington, but he didn't know where they had gone. The doctor and the some of the local men were getting Thompson, Taylor, Ferguson, and Jackson to the road, where an old truck was waiting. For the first time, it was noticed that Loren Zimmer, the right waist gunner, was nowhere to be seen, nor had he been present since the crash. Before Rawlings or Finley could consider that oddity, or where Don and Jim had gone, the two boys were pointing to a patch of woods up a hill and across a gully, then they were pointing to the approaching vehicle which appeared to be a German army truck. Thinking about their fellow crewmen wasn't an option, and the two airmen ran as fast as they could toward the woods, trying to put as much distance between them and the crash site as possible. Fueled by pure adrenalin, the two men made it to the woods and collapsed from exhaustion. They dared not move for fear of someone seeing them. To make matters worse, there was a German aircraft circling the area of the village.

They noticed smoke rising from the crash site. Nothing seemed to make sense to the two men as they hid in the underbrush deep in the patch of trees.

They thought that their watches must be lying. How could they have only been shot down a few minutes ago? It seemed like the day had been so long, but it was just a few hours since they had taken off on the mission to Frankfurt. Then they had the engine problems, and then the Messerschmitt attack and the dive toward the clouds. When the clouds ran out, the two Focke Wulfs had shown up, then everything seemed to happen so fast.

And where *were* they? The boy said Belgium, but *where* in Belgium? How can we run for our lives if we don't know which way to run? And where was the rest of the crew?

Thompson, Taylor, Ferguson, and Jackson were badly wounded, but accounted for. But where had Fowler, Arrington and Dinwiddie gone? And Zimmer? He wasn't at the crash site, so where could he be?

The questions were many, and the answers few. At this point in time, January 29, 1944, just after one o'clock in the afternoon, the men of the Fowler crew became separated. Some of the crew members would see others from the crew occasionally over the next few days and weeks, but the crew as a whole ceased to exist. It would be several decades before the mystery of what had happened to each of them after that winter day in 1944. They had departed England afraid, but still sure that they would be returning that afternoon to Molesworth with another mission in the logbook. They were so sure of their success that they had voted to fly the mission with one sick engine. Then came the flak, the blown #4 engine, the Me-109s and the Focke Wulfs. The reality of the war had eroded their bravado. In just a few minutes after hitting that field somewhere in Belgium, their lives would change forever, and the irony was that not one member of the crew would know the entire story during their lifetimes. Some thought they did, but again, all the facts had not come together until the last surviving member of the crew had passed away. In fact, there are still mysteries regarding some of the crew members of the *G.I. Sheets* after that fateful mission to Frankfurt. In the following chapters, the events of the post-crash lives of the crew members will be discussed, using all the available information available in 2020.

chapter four

EVASION

Despite the bad decision not to abort the mission as soon as the failing supercharger was discovered, and the bad fortune that put the *G.I. Sheets* and the Fowler crew on the ground, there was an element of very good luck at play. Short of landing somewhere back in the United Kingdom, Belgium was the best of all possibilities for a forced landing. Popping out of the clouds directly over a German Luftwaffe field was certainly bad luck, but the pilots who shot them down actually let them land. And the village near where they landed was a piece of excellent good fortune.

The area in which they crash landed was in southern Belgium near the French border. The largest town near them was Beaumont, with a population of nearly 7,500 in 2020. About four kilometers (two and one-half miles) to the southeast of Beaumont is the village of Solre Saint Gery, and about the same distance from Solre Saint Gery to the northeast is the smaller village of Barbencon. By lucky happenstance, within the population of these three towns were several individuals who were very involved in the Belgian resistance, and had been active in hiding and moving downed Allied aviators since Belgium had fallen to the Germans in 1940. In addition, the location was near enough to the French border that it was relatively easy to communicate and operate with the French resistance cells.

The exploits of the French resistance in World War II is legendary, but the Belgian partisans were just as aggressive in their endeavors to thwart the Germans who occupied their country. The Belgians had a small advantage in that theirs is a multilingual country. In the northern part of Belgium, Dutch (Flemish) is a commonly spoken language. In the east, near the border with Germany, one commonly hears German. And in the south, near France, the prevalent language is French. These languages tend to blend, and it is not unusual to hear parts of all three languages being commonly used. Belgians have been referred to as "the chameleons of Europe" because they can often blend into any of the three neighboring countries, depending upon their language skills. The American OSS (Office of Strategic Services, forerunner of the Central Intelligence Agency) and the British Ministry of Intelligence capitalized on this trait. A good Belgian "spy" could operate in a wide area of Western Europe.

As was mentioned in the last chapter, when the crew made their forced landing near the village of Solre Saint Gery, they had no idea where they were.

Additionally, if one adds that into the mix of adrenalin and fear from what had happened to them during the last few hours, the fact that most had been wounded to various degrees, and one of their friends was killed, it is understandable that they had conflicting memories over the years about what had actually occurred. Because of the quick action of the members of the Belgian underground, they were quickly sequestered from each other, and after the crash and until almost four decades later, not one individual could relate what had happened to any of his fellow crew members. The Fowler crew didn't know it, but the Belgians of Solre Saint Gery were planning their fate before they ever touched down in the muddy field (locally named Marly's Field) on the edge of the village. Because of their ties to the underground, they knew what to do if an airman dropped in on them. In this case, it was an entire plane and crew.

The time was about 12:45, and most of the people of Solre Saint Gery had just finished eating their noon meal. Many were clearing their tables when the sound of a large plane in trouble could be heard. They were accustomed to hearing large aircraft flying over at higher altitudes, but this one was down low, and from the sound of it, was having engine problems. Mixed with the sound of the large plane was the familiar sound of a German fighter plane. And there were the sounds of machine guns. Everyone who heard the sounds of the aircraft rushed outside to see what was going on.

Sylvie Lecouturier-Derenne, owner of a beauty shop in the village, was one who rushed out into the street and saw the large bomber headed for the open field on the higher ground near the limestone quarry. The engines were smoking, and trailing the large plane was a Focke Wulf fighter. She ran back inside to her telephone and called Dr. Maurice Verstraeten. Besides being the local physician, he was also the leader of the local cell of the Comet Line. The Comet Line was an organization in the Belgian underground with the purpose of hiding and moving Allied fliers. Because he was the local doctor and needed to be able to visit patients, the Germans had approved him to use his motor scooter, and even gave him a gasoline ration in order to make his rounds. It is ironic that the Germans were also funding his travel expenses in order to run his branch of the Comet Line.

On the street with Sylvie and also watching the aircraft was her younger teenaged brother, Arthur Derenne. When he had an idea of where the plane would crash, Arthur took off at a run to go to the site.

He covered the distance in about six or seven minutes but stopped short of the crashed bomber to carefully assess who was there. Dr. Verstraeten was slipping and sliding across the muddy field on his motor scooter, and he also spied Father Robert near the crashed plane. That was good. They were the right people to be there, and there were no Germans in sight… yet. He heard someone letting out a loud whistle and saw his friend Emile Mourue down the slope of the hill near some bushes. Emile was waving him to come down to where he was standing. Arthur trotted over and found three of the American aviators hiding under the bushes. We know now that the three airmen had to have been Don Dinwiddie, Jim Fowler, and Richard Arrington. The German fighter plane had been circling the area, and Emile, also a resistance member, had quickly maneuvered the men away from the crashed plane and into hiding.

Once the three Americans had been sheltered in the bushes, Arthur ran up the hill to the bomber, which was now on fire. Dr. Verstraeten was treating the three wounded men (obviously Taylor, Thompson, and Ferguson), and another of the crew was lying off to himself, obviously dead (Miller Jackson), and Father Paul Robert was ministering to him.

Standing behind the priest was ten-year-old Marcel Devergnies. When Marcel saw Arthur approaching, he ran to him. Together he and Arthur went to the two crewmen (Rawlings and Finley) who were standing near the doctor. One was wounded slightly, and had blood on his face, but the other looked unharmed. They seemed dazed and puzzled about what was going on around them, but the unhurt man was trying to speak French to him, and doing a terrible job of it. He pointed at the ground, and Arthur figured out that he didn't know where they were. Arthur told him that they were in Belgium.

Marcel grabbed Arthur's arm and pointed off in the distance. From the slight rise where they were standing, they could see the barely visible vehicle approaching. It looked like a German truck, and it wouldn't take it long to get there. Arthur tried to tell the Americans that the Germans were coming, probably alerted by the Focke Wulf pilots. The truck was probably from the observation tower at the cross roads near Vergnies, about seven kilometers away, because it was the nearest German outpost. Arthur pointed to the group of trees off in the distance, across a gully and up another hill. Finally, the two aviators understood that they should run to the trees and hide. Co-pilot Barney Rawlings and engineer Curt Finley took off at a run toward the woods.

While they were trying to convince the two Americans to run, they hadn't noticed that a truck had pulled up on the road near the crash site. There were several people coming and going from the crash at this point, and the truck that had arrived was Maurice Lamendin of the nearby village of Clermont. Several of the village residents were helping the three wounded men (Joseph Thompson, Alvin Taylor, and Jack Ferguson) to the truck to be transported to the nearest hospital. Several of the men were helping to carry the body of Miller Jackson to the truck. Dr. Verstraeten had questioned the Americans about whether or not they wanted to go to the hospital, or to be hidden by people in the village. To go to the hospital would be a certain trip to a German prison camp at some later date, because the Germans would be taking custody of them after they were admitted. Taylor and Ferguson opted for the hospital, but Thompson, although seriously wounded, suddenly decided not to go. Thompson was hustled off to the home of another resistance member just before the German truck made its way to the crash site. Dr. Verstraeten went to the three men hiding in the bushes, had a few words with them in English, then went back to the crash site after making sure the men were well hidden. He also made sure that all of the parachutes in the bomber were taken away to be destroyed except for three that could be attributed to the two men going to the hospital and the man who was dead.

The small truck was driven by a lone German soldier coming to inspect the crashed plane. He spoke to Dr. Verstraeten, saw the two wounded men and the dead man, and asked where the rest of the crew was. Of course, everyone plead ignorance of seeing anyone other than the three men at hand. The young soldier asked to see Dr. Verstraeten's credentials, and when he saw that he had been approved by the occupying German army to act as a local physician, he seemed satisfied. He gave the bomber a cursory look, but it was smoldering from the fire, and he didn't linger. The attempt to destroy the bomber had failed, and only one wing and the tail were destroyed, and the rest was still more or less intact. The Norden bombsight had been destroyed in the attack by the Messerschmitts near Frankfurt, and Don Dinwiddie had destroyed the mission code book, but there was one bit of equipment that created a bit of concern.

According to Dr. Verstraeten, while he was treating Jack Ferguson's wounds, Ferguson told him that he had removed a small device from the plane called the IFF box. The IFF ("Identification, Friend or Foe") device was able to send a special signal that identified a friendly aircraft to Allied defenses so that it wouldn't be attacked by fighters when approaching home in bad weather or at night. It sent it a coded signal in response to being hit by Allied radar beamed from the ground.

While not in the "top secret" league with the Norden bombsight, it was nonetheless an important piece of equipment. If it fell into enemy hands, theoretically it could be used to disguise a German aircraft as a friendly plane, allowing it to sneak in at night and bomb Allied installations. The likelihood of that actually happening was slight, because the IFF responded with a special code that was changed often, usually daily. The chances of the Germans being able to use the device at that point in the war was practically nil, because the technology was much more advanced than it was in the earlier days of radar.

For reasons unknown, Ferguson supposedly had in his possession the IFF from the crashed B-17. Since he was wounded and had to make his way forward from his tail gun position to the exit aft of the radioman's compartment, maybe he saw it, and reacted from being previously trained to disable it so that it wouldn't fall into enemy hands. Why Don Dinwiddie hadn't removed it is unknown, but as was mentioned earlier, it was no longer a top-secret device in 1944, so it probably wasn't a priority after the crash. Ferguson did have it, though, and he passed it on to Dr. Verstraeten as the doctor was giving him aid after the crash. Just after Verstraeten received it and hid it in his pants, the lone German soldier showed up in the truck that had earlier been seen on its way to the crash site. The doctor was afraid there would be trouble.

The young German had come from the observation tower a few miles away near the town of Vergnies. By the time he had arrived, all of the crewmen were gone except for the deceased Miller Jackson, Jack Ferguson, and Alvin Taylor, and it was a relief that the German didn't seem too interested in what was going on. He gave the plane a cursory inspection and checked Dr. Verstraeten's official credentials. As he was looking at his papers that gave him German approval for having the motor bike and the right to be there, he was being watched by one of the other bystanders. Dr. Verstraeten saw the Belgian man, who was the town constable, open his coat to display to the doctor that he had a handgun, and would use it on the German if there was trouble. It never came to that, and after the young soldier saw that the crew was gone, that the dead and wounded were being transported, he seemed satisfied. The plane was smoldering, as the fire hadn't consumed it as the villagers had hoped, but it was enough that the German seemed to want to leave the crash and head back to his observation tower to report his findings. All thought it was strange that only one soldier came, and even he wasn't all that interested in the American bomber or its crew.

From all of the theatrics we have seen in old war movies, it would be expected that the Germans would have shown up en masse, searching door to door for the escaped crew members, but that wasn't happening. Only three crew members were found at the crash, and one of them was deceased. The Germans certainly knew that the normal crew of a B-17 was a minimum of ten men. Why were they seemingly uninterested in finding the crew members that were not accounted for? There were at least two reasons for their actions, and once again, only after the passage of time since the war have the facts become more clearly understood. The Germans *were* interested in the crew, but not for the obvious reasons.

It was mentioned earlier that the Fowler crew couldn't have found a better place to have been forced down than the field outside of Solre Saint Gery. The area was the home of several Belgian resistance members working with more than one "cell" or escape line. The forced landing of the *G.I. Sheets* and the disappearance of most of its crew was a fortunate event for the Germans as well as the bomber crew. But why did the German response to the crash seem to show such disinterest?

The first reason is very simple: the Germans weren't really interested in capturing the crew members. The enemy had learned long before that the average bomber crew member was just a man carrying out his orders, and didn't possess any serious military secrets or knowledge. A captured bomber crewman would be given a brief interrogation, then sent to a prison camp. They had lots of Allied POW's to house and feed as it was, and they were not in a hurry to find more. If they discovered them, they would follow the process of interrogating and locking them in a Stalag, but they wouldn't expend a great deal of effort to do so.

The second reason that the Germans weren't in a hurry to catch the crewmen is that they were using them as bait. The Germans were very much aware of the activities of the Dutch, Belgian, and French underground cells. They knew that they were sneaking downed aviators out of the occupied territories, and they apprehended partisans as they discovered them. But the real problem to the Germans wasn't the exfiltration of downed aviators. The troublesome part of the underground organizations was the infiltration of Allied operatives. This organized system that was helping downed aviators to escape could also work very well to bring Allied spies and other operatives into the German-held territories.

The Nazis were aware that there would soon be a land invasion by massive Allied forces. They were also very aware of the fact that the Allies were definitely aiding the underground organizations of the occupied territories. Although the Germans didn't know the extent of this, the American Office of Strategic Services (O.S.S.) and the British Intelligence Service were planning a secret program called Operation Jedburgh. In this operation, agents and supplies were to be secretly dropped by parachute into certain areas in order to aid the underground shortly before the Allied land invasion would occur. The Jedburgh agents were to be dropped at night from special aircraft that flew with the British bombers on their night bombing attacks. During any bombing raid, it was common for some aircraft to develop problems that would force them to drop out of formation and make a run back toward England. Aircraft that had been specially modified to allow drops of personnel and equipment would follow the bombers toward Germany, but would mimic a bomber in trouble and turn back toward the west, dropping in altitude. The navigator and pilot on these aircraft would locate the clandestine drop zone, and flying at a very low altitude, would make the insertion. The aircraft would stay at the very low altitude all the way back to the English Channel. Changes in the ideas and methodology of these clandestine drops will be explored in greater detail later in this book.

For the Allies to pull off such a large invasion, they needed to know details of German troop placements, transportation routes, etc. What better way to know about such things than having actual boots on the ground? British and American agents had been infiltrating Europe to scout out such objectives, and also making contacts with members of the resistance. The Germans were constantly trying to infiltrate and destroy this pipeline that was helping to bring Allied agents into their occupied areas, and when the *G.I. Sheets* crashed in the field at Solre Saint Gery, its presence was put to use. What happened was a cat-and-mouse game that none of the Fowler crew and few of the local resistance workers were aware of until it was too late to counter.

In actuality, it appears that the Germans were waiting for a situation that had befallen the Fowler crew on the *G.I. Sheets*. An aircraft that suffered a crash landing with most of the crew surviving was the perfect scenario for putting into operation a plan to try to root out members of the Belgian underground. Through a lucky phone call that Dr. Verstraeten had received just moments before he was notified about the crashed bomber at Solre Saint Gery, the local members of the resistance were forewarned of possible German snooping and were exercising extra caution.

Just minutes before receiving the call from Sylvie about the bomber, Dr. Verstraeten had a call from Louis Hautier of the village of Barbencon, which was just a few miles east of Solre Saint Gery. Hautier was also a member of the resistance and said that an American aviator from a crashed plane had wandered into town. The aviator was in his flying gear, was handing out English cigarettes and food to the locals, and was asking to be taken to the local resistance workers in order to be sheltered. And he spoke very good French.

When Verstraeten reached the crash site, there was one man missing, with only nine men accounted for. After he had treated Ferguson and dealt with the dying Jackson, he was waiting for Maurice Lamendin to arrive with his truck to transport the severely wounded to the hospital. While he waited, he was with three of the crew as they were hiding in some bushes near the road, below the hill where the plane had gone down. One of the men was the pilot of the aircraft. The men, of course, were Fowler, Arrington, and Dinwiddie. The doctor took the opportunity to talk to them. He asked how many men were on the crew. Fowler confirmed that there were ten. He asked about the missing man.

Don told him about Zimmer jumping out at a very low altitude just before the airplane landed in the field. He revealed that he saw Zimmer jump up and head for the escape hatch when the bailout bell rang to warn of the impending hard landing. He lunged toward him, but he couldn't get to Zimmer in time to restrain him. Don was sure that he had probably jumped to his death at such a low altitude.

"How far away from here did he jump?" asked Verstraeten, who knew that the plane had come from the east, maybe over or near Barbencon.

"No more than thirty seconds before we hit the field," said Dinwiddie.

"Did the man who jumped speak French?"asked the doctor. Fowler assured him that he did not.

Verstraeten knew that the man in Barbencon could not be the missing man from the Fowler crew. A man jumping that low before the plane crash landed probably *didn't* survive, and even if by some miracle he had lived, he couldn't have made the trip to Barbencon that quickly. The doctor knew that the man whom Hautier had called about had to be from another downed American plane, or an imposter. Later, after getting the wounded to the hospital and the other survivors hidden among the homes of the various resistance members, he called Hautier to warn him about the man. Hautier didn't want to believe him and decided to introduce the downed "aviator" to members of a resistance cell in Clermont. A few days later the German Gestapo descended on the Clermont area and arrested twenty-three citizens who were linked to the Belgian underground. They were taken away and never seen again. The end result was that Dr. Verstraeten and his fellow resistance members had to be extra diligent in keeping the movements of the Fowler crew secret.

If the Germans had a plan in place to take advantage of a crashed plane that could be that quickly implemented, it was certain that they had other spies and observers around, be they Belgian or German.

Maurice Lamendin arrived with his truck, and he and Dr. Verstraeten and another villager, Vincent Vincent, loaded Taylor, Ferguson, and the body of Miller Jackson in the back of the truck. Vincent rode in the bed of the truck with the three Americans, and this gave Dr. Verstraeten the opportunity to speak alone with Lamendin as they drove. They were both concerned about the fact that too many people knew about the aviators, and they both knew that not everyone in town could be trusted. The crew had been dispersed to different locations.

Fowler and Dinwiddie were hidden in a stable, Arrington had been taken to Sylvie's beauty shop, and Thompson, who refused to go to the hospital, was hiding in the home of Anna Bouvigne-Lecouturier, which was next door to the Verstraeten residence. Rawlings and Finley were last seen running to the patch of woods just before the German soldier showed up, and nobody knew where Zimmer was, but he was feared dead. Verstraeten and Lamendin decided that upon returning from the hospital, they would move the airmen to different locations with as much secrecy as possible. On the way to the hospital they made a quick stop at Dr. Verstraeten's home for the purpose of disposing of the IFF device. Before leaving his house for the hospital, the doctor asked Taylor and Ferguson once more if they were sure that they preferred going to the hospital over going to private homes, and they both reaffirmed that they wanted medical attention. Off to the hospital they went, into the waiting hands of the Germans who would be taking charge of them.

It must be remembered that by early 1944, at the time of the crash of the Fowler crew, the Belgian, Dutch, and French underground movements had been at work for almost four years. Considering that they were operating under the very noses of the German occupation, they were exceedingly efficient at hiding and moving downed aviators. They also knew, for the most part, who the suspected traitors were in their communities, and also those who were gossips and couldn't be trusted with clandestine information. As was mentioned before, the area of Beaumont/Solre Saint Gery/Barbencon was a veritable crossroads of resistance cells or "lines". The Comet Line, one of the oldest escape/evasion operations, was represented in the area, as well as the "Group G" and the "Marc Line".

Unlike the more discreet French Resistance, it was not uncommon for Belgian partisans to belong to more than one line. Dr. Verstraeten was the local head of both the Comet Line and the Marc Line. The local head of the Group G was Father Paul Robert. Because what they did was clandestine, there was not a lot of visible structure to their organization. There was, however, a chain of command. Above the local head of the lines was an area "commander", in this case it was Rene Hannecart of Beaumont. Orders and instructions would come down from him, and he was dealing with higher level contacts in the Allied forces and the Belgian government in exile. In all likelihood, he was probably in possession of a shortwave radio in which he could communicate with Allied contacts in London, and if not, he certainly was given ever-changing code words that he would be able to hear on commercial British radio that would clandestinely tell him of secret drops of equipment and possibly Allied operatives.

The Comet Line was the forerunner of all the escape lines. It was the idea of a twenty-four-year-old Belgian woman by the name of Andree de Jongh. She had friends who lived on the border between France and the neutral Spain in the Pyrenees Mountains, and envisioned a system of "friends" who would move downed airmen from Belgium, through France, and into Spain, and then on to England. The plan was brilliant and worked well enough that over 800 airmen were smuggled out of German-held territory by the end of the war. De Jongh and her network worked very closely with British Intelligence and the American Office of Strategic Services, (which after the war morphed into the current

Central Intelligence Agency). The Germans knew of the escape lines but had extreme difficulty in breaking them. The lines were made up of civilians who were familiar with their respective geographical areas, and they operated with the utmost secrecy. As with the episode of Hautier, sometimes portions, or cells, were broken, but the cells were isolated enough from one another that this was difficult to do.

Within the structure of the resistance there were groups with special skills or assignments. Dr. Verstraeten and his companions were charged with hiding and moving downed aviators (and perhaps Allied operatives?). There was another part of the resistance that was an underground "army", and their job was the sabotage and destruction of German infrastructure and transportation. This group was the A.S., "armee sous-terrain", or "underground Army".

The members of the A.S. were also responsible for weeding out the suspected infiltrators. Before the incident of the "fake airman" claiming to be from the crash of the *G.I. Sheets*, there had been other such infiltrators.

Once enough information had been gathered to show that the person was probably a German agent, he was quickly and quietly eliminated. The most bitter pill for the resistance workers to swallow was the fact that some of their own countrymen were Nazi sympathizers.

In dealing with that kind of problem, the person sometimes quietly disappeared, or died in an "accident". After the Allied liberation in the months after D-Day, many of those suspected of collaborating with the Germans were quickly rounded up by the members of the resistance and handed over to the authorities.

Another problem was the close proximity to the French border. Nazi collaborators from France were known to cross the border into southern Belgium posing as simple travelers or tradesmen in order to gather information for the Germans. The fact that French was the common language in southwestern Belgium greatly aided this endeavor. The Belgian resistance was on the lookout for such people, but as can be seen by the incident with the fake aviator in Barbencon, even seasoned resistance members like Louis Hautier could be fooled.

After dropping Taylor and Ferguson at the hospital, Verstraeten, Lamenden, and Vincent made an uneventful return to Solre Saint Gery.

Later that night, they started moving the members of the Fowler crew to new locations. Verstraeton moved navigator Joe Thompson from the home of Anna Bouvigne-Lecouturier to his house. He felt that Thompson, with metal and plexiglass splinters in his face and eyes, needed close medical attention, so staying at the doctor's home would be best for him. Lamenden picked up Fowler and Dinwiddie from the stable and took them to his home and hid them in his barn. Arrington was taken out of the Sylvie's beauty shop and into the Liqueux home in Beaumont.

The next day brought good news in the form of Albert Rolin, a local farmer. Rolin showed up at Verstraeten's home with the missing Loren Zimmer, who was miraculously alive. Zimmer had jumped at a ridiculously low altitude, and his chute had time to only partially open. The streaming chute had slowed his descent somewhat and pulled him into an upright position. He had the excellent fortune to land feet-first into a soft, muddy bog on Rolin's farm, which Rolin witnessed. He immediately got to Zimmer, pulled him out of the mud, and hid him on his property for the rest of the day and night. After checking in with Verstraeten, Zimmer was taken to Maurice Lamendin's residence, and Fowler and Dinwiddie were relieved and thrilled to see that their friend had survived his jump.

During the next few days after the crash of their bomber, Fowler, Dinwiddie, Arrington, and Zimmer were moved frequently. Thompson, because of his wounds, was moved, but always kept close to Dr. Verstraeten.

The Germans had been doing a cursory search of the area, but there were no close calls, and after a few days, the searching ended. As mentioned earlier, they were probably more interested in the resistance workers than the downed aviators. The men were moved frequently in the first few weeks, then settled into more permanent locations after it seemed that the Germans had lost interest in looking for them.

Don Dinwiddie and Jim Fowler were moved to the home of Maurice Lamendin's grandmother, Madame Hermance Miot, which was just north of the town of Thirimont, several kilometers north of Beaumont. They were visited daily by a farm family, the Quertaimonts, who brought their meals each night at midnight. Sylvie Derenne visited, sometimes with her apprentice, nineteen-year-old Anne-Marie Bouffault, to cut their hair and deliver messages. The two men stayed inside during the day, only venturing out during darkness.

Richard Arrington had been placed with Sylvie and her husband Carme in the early days after the crash, then was moved for a time into the home of Anne-Marie and her family. He was later moved from there to the home of Valentine Tilmant, a widow in Beaumont.

Joe Thompson, after being moved several times in the early days, finally came to the home of Etienne Devergnies at Leugnies. A physician by the name of Biernaux from Lodelinsart had a second home there and attempted to remove a troublesome metal splinter from Thompson's eye, but wasn't successful. Her advice was to wait until he could have a more thorough surgery when he was returned to the United States.

Dr. Biernaux, along with Dr. Verstraeten, continued to give medical care to all the hidden aviators during her frequent stays in the Beaumont area. It must be remembered that all of them had been wounded to some extent during the Frankfurt mission, and Thompson was the most seriously wounded of those who were still evading. Taylor and Ferguson were immediately taken into custody by the Germans after being delivered to the hospital, and remained there until well enough to be transferred to a prison camp. Taylor later said that he was happy with the medical care he had received at the hands of both the Belgian and German doctors while in the hospital.

Loren Zimmer remained at the home of Maurice Lamendin. Also, at Lamendin's home was a British aviator, John Leyne, pilot of a Halifax bomber flown out of RAF Croft in England. He had to bail out of his disabled aircraft on a night bombing mission and had connected with the Belgian underground.

Not accounted for were top turret gunner/engineer Curtis Finley and copilot Barney Rawlings. They were last seen running to hide in a patch of woods away from the crash site. Their whereabouts were not known, and it was certain that they were not in the Solre Saint Gery area or the word would have filtered down to the leaders of the resistance. Maybe they were captured by the Germans. Maybe they were on their way to Spain. Nobody knew, but everyone hoped for the best.

Another nagging thought plagued all of the survivors: what were their families back home thinking? The crew would be listed as

Missing In Action after their failure to return from the mission on January 29.

The MIA label was scary, almost tantamount to saying, "we don't know what happened to them, but they're probably dead" to most of the family members back home. In actuality, MIA meant that they were either missing, taken prisoner, evading capture, or killed. Until any of those possibilities were confirmed, they were listed as officially Missing In Action. When the crew failed to return from the Frankfurt mission, any returning crews from that mission who might possess any information about the Fowler crew and/or their assigned aircraft were supposed to give that information to the interviewing officers at the post-mission debriefing. Barring any confirmation that the Fowler crew or their plane was destroyed, after confirming that it had not returned to another airfield in the U.K., a Missing Air Crew Report (known as a MACR) was opened, and any future information coming in about the crew was entered into that document. The document was open until the confirmation of the whereabouts of all crew members.

On February 12, 1944, two weeks after the disappearance of the Fowler crew, Archie and Irma Dinwiddie, parents of Don, received a telegram notifying them of their son's MIA status.

The telegram attempted to carry a note of optimism, saying that the crew's status could not be confirmed, and that to remain hopeful that they would hear good news in the near future. The telegram also promised that more news would be sent immediately upon learning anything in the future.

The first glimmer of hope came a few weeks later through the "grapevine" network of the crew's families. Word came from the International Red Cross to the family of bombardier Alvin Taylor that he had been wounded, but had been cared for and was in the custody of the Germans as a POW. His family relayed that information to the other crew families, because if Al had survived, perhaps the others had, too. It was the first good news that they had to hang onto. The crew members who were hiding out though the efforts of the Belgians had no way of getting word to the families or to the Allied forces of their survival, but hoped that if Al and Jack Ferguson were taken prisoner by the Germans at the hospital, word would officially be sent to their families by the Red Cross. What they had *hoped* would happen, *had* happened. They just had no way of knowing that.

Over the next several months things settled into a routine, although hiding in the enemy's occupied territory could never be "routine".

The men were all separated and hidden, and the news of the war filtered in to them from various sources. It seemed that the land invasion of western Europe had to be coming soon. Allied bombers seemed to be overhead night and day. Endless streams could be seen headed eastward toward German targets.

How long could the enemy hold out under such a massive bombing campaign? The Germans had come to the crash site of their B-17 to scavenge the gasoline left in the left wing tanks, which had failed to be destroyed by the fire. If they were that desperate for fuel, they could not be faring well. The downed aviators knew from the few missions that they had flown that German air defenses had been getting weaker in France and Belgium, and stronger in Germany. Were the Germans pulling back, going into a defensive stance? All signs pointed to a land invasion that would happen sooner rather than later.

The imminent Allied land invasion also changed the operational plans of some of the escape lines. The normal operation was the eventual movement of the downed aviators south, through France, over the Pyrenees Mountains, then into neutral Spain.

From there the escaped aviators would go to Gibralter, then would be flown home to England. Alternately, and more risky, was moving the evadees to the coast of France, then across the English Channel in the middle of the night in a fast boat sent from England.

Shortly after the Fowler crash, the philosophy seemed to change. Instead of moving the evading men, it now seemed that they were sheltering in place. The rationale was that if the invasion was coming soon, hiding the evadees might be of less risk than trying to move them. This philosophy seemed to be the plan of action being followed in the spring of 1944 with the evading crew members of the *G.I. Sheets*. They all seemed to be doing well in hiding, and the Germans, though present, seemed to be not overly interested in looking for downed aviators. On the night of April 13, 1944, everything changed.

On that night, several Gestapo agents came to the home of Dr. Verstraeten and searched it thoroughly. They seemed to be looking for something or someone in particular. Rene Bouvigne, an eighteen-year-old college student who traveled to Chimay from Beaumont daily for classes, acted as a courier for the resistance. He was sleeping in the attic of the house he shared with his widowed mother and younger sister.

He was awakened by noises from below, and looked out the window to see his mother and sister being taken from their house to the home of Dr. Verstraeten across the street. He expected the Gestapo to come search their house, but they did not. He watched all night long and could tell that whatever was happening concerned the Verstraeten's, but he couldn't understand why his mother and sister had been taken there.

His mother had hidden evading airmen in their home, and his sister, even as young as she was, had carried messages to and from other resistance members. He himself was very involved, carrying messages and items (the IFF being one) back and forth to Chimay on his daily commute to school. They evidently weren't looking for him or didn't know about him. All night long he watched the coming and going of Gestapo next door, then all was quiet; his mother and sister came home about 6:00 a.m. as the Gestapo left.

From what his mother had told him, the Gestapo had a tip that Dr. Verstraeten was hiding a downed aviator in his home, but they found no evidence of that. They questioned his mother and sister about what they had seen and had thoroughly searched the Verstraeten house. Whatever they were looking for, it apparently was very specific in nature. When they found nothing, they left. It was somewhat ironic in that downed airmen had frequently been hidden at the Bouvigne home, but the Gestapo had never searched there. It was obvious that they were being tipped off by someone who knew Verstraeten had been caring for some of the Fowler crew.

What Verstraeten and the Bouvignes were not aware of at the time was that while the group of Gestapo agents were searching the Verstraeten home, two other groups of Gestapo had gone to the home of Carme and Sylvie Derenne-Lecouturier as well as the home of her young apprentice, Anne-Marie Bouffault.

We know now what had happened to initiate this raid. Apparently when Richard Arrington was placed in the home of Carme and Sylvie, Anne-Marie was privy to this. In fact, Arrington was placed for a short time with Anne-Marie's family. Anne-Marie's mother was friends with a man named Amboise Boudart from the town of Merbes-le-Chateau. Boudart made statements to the Bouffault family that made them think he was with the resistance, and when this information was relayed to Verstraeten, he knew that this was not true. Verstraeten immediately removed Arrington from Sylvie's house and hoped that was the end of the problem. In retrospect, it was ascertained later that Boudart was an informer for the Germans, and was responsible for the arrests of Carme, Sylvie, and Anna-Marie and the unsuccessful raid on Verstraeten's home.

Carme and Sylvie were immediately arrested by the Germans, tried in a tribunal and sentenced to death for aiding the enemy. The husband and wife were separated and moved several times to different prisons. They were fortunate that the liberation of Belgium came before their death sentences were carried out. Carme was liberated by the Americans in February of 1945, and Sylvie by the Russians on May 6, 1945.

In an interview with Sylvie at her home in Solre Saint Gery in 1988, I asked her if she felt any ill will toward the Germans today for her treatment during the war. "No", she said with a smile. "Different times, different people". I'm not certain that most people would have been so forgiving, but Sylvie knew it was the Nazis, not all Germans, that had taken her.

No record has been found of what became of Anna-Marie, but in the absence of the discovery of any charges or punishment, the assumption is that she was released by the Germans.

As for the person of Amboise Boudart, he was immediately arrested after the liberation of Belgium by the Allies. His association with other Belgian and French Nazi collaborators was investigated and over time, several individuals were apprehended and punished.

In discussing enemy collaborators, there are a couple of reasons this occurred in most cases. Either the person was collaborating with the Nazis because they were afraid to stand against them, or they were believers in the Nazi ideals and were eager to work for them.

Having their country taken over by an oppressive enemy could make some people do things that they wouldn't ordinarily do, and not having been in that situation it is difficult for most of us to understand. After the war there was a large effort to track down and prosecute known collaborators in Belgium and France. Later in this book the topic will be discussed in more detail and examined in regard to how it applied to some of the Fowler crew.

After the Gestapo raid on the Verstraeten house and the arrest of Sylvie and Carme, there were definite changes in the operation of the resistance network in the Beaumont area. The men were watched closer by their handlers, and the contact they had with others was more restricted. Oddly enough, after that night, there was no further attempt by the Germans to root out any of the resistance workers or any hidden aviators.

May 1944 brought two major changes for the men of the Fowler crew. The biggest news came to the men's families back home, but the evadees in Belgium had no knowledge of it. Barney Rawlings, whose situation had been unknown since he and Finley had run away from the crash to hide in the woods on January 29, had made it out of Belgium, through France, over the Pyrenees Mountains and into Spain. After hiding in the woods during the afternoon of the crash, he and Curt Finley had a disagreement over the best course of action that they should follow. Finley felt that they should leave the woods immediately, but Rawlings felt that it would be best to stay there during the night and move later. Rather than try to pull rank on Finley or try to force him to stay in place, they shook hands, Rawlings wished him well, and Curt departed.

The next morning Barney started his journey, first stopping at a farmhouse that was inhabited by a family that were happy to feed him and give him civilian clothing.

After getting back on the road and heading south, he used the same method to find help. He tried to avoid larger towns, and looked for farmhouses, and tried to avoid anything threatening. He was finally connected to the resistance workers in the French underground, and they took him in and guided him all the way to Gibralter, thence to England. It's interesting to note that when he was moved into Paris by the underground, he ran into Curt Finley, who had been following basically the same plan as Barney and who had also connected with the underground. Both of them were given forged documents and better clothing to help them fool the Germans if they were stopped.

They traveled together to the Pyrenees Mountains led by guides working for the French underground, but again, Finley disagreed with the plan just short of the Spanish border and went a different direction. He was captured by the Germans just a few kilometers from freedom and ended up in a POW camp for the remainder of the war. Rawlings made it into Spain, then to Gibraltar, and was back in England on May 23, 1944.

Rawlings' return to England was good news for all the families. Official word was finally sent to the families that on the day of the crash, all crew members were alive except for Miller Jackson. The copilot confirmed that Thompson, Taylor, and Ferguson were seriously wounded and were headed to the hospital when he last saw them. This, of course, was in error, because Thompson decided to stay in private care and did not go to the hospital. At any rate, for the families back home the news was good at this point.

The only problem was that if the men had survived the crash, where were they? The families of the men could only hope and pray that they were well and in hiding, because if they were prisoners, the Germans had failed to notify the International Red Cross as they were obligated to do. The only other possibility was that if they were not in hiding, and the Germans didn't have them, then they were killed after Rawlings left the group. The fact that there was no news was good in that they hadn't been captured, but it was bad because of the unknown possibilities inherent in being on the run in a country occupied by the enemy. But the word coming to the families regarding Barney's successful escape gave hope where there was very little before.

Don and Jim had seen Thompson, Arrington, and Zimmer in late March. Since then, they had been alone in the home of Mrs. Miot at Thirimont. There was little news of the other men except the sparse information relayed by resistance members who dropped by with food, medical care, or to give them haircuts. It must have been a scary bit of news when they found out about Sylvie and her husband getting taken away by the Gestapo.

Sylvie was deeply involved in the Belgian resistance movement, and she knew where Dinwiddie and Fowler were being held. She had even sheltered Don in her attic for a period of time. After she was arrested on April 13, Don and Jim were no doubt waiting for the Germans to raid their hiding place. In spite of the change in underground plans from moving the evadees to having them stay in place until the land invasion, the two men were getting impatient at hiding and started to feel like they should be moving.

Adding to their fear of discovery, shortly after the Gestapo raid on Verstraeten's home and the capture of Sylvie and her husband, a group of German soldiers showed up in front of Miot's home. They apparently were getting loud with each other for some reason, and Madame Miot went out of her house and yelled at them to leave, that they were annoying her. Incredibly, they left, but the presence of the Germans seemed to spur on the thoughts of moving the airmen before someone decided to search the house. Thirimont was barely a kilometer from the border with France. They were no doubt thinking about leaving and taking their chances on trying to make it to England.

Father Paul Robert, the local leader of the Group G resistance cell, and also the priest that was at the crash site, was consulted. The men were moved immediately, even though it took several days to get all of the travel details completed.

On April 14, the two men left Madame Miot's home and were transported to the village of Clermont (about nine kilometers) by Maurice Lamendin. They spent the night at the residence of Nelly Quertin. With her as a guide, Don and Jim left with her on bicycles for the trip to Solre Saint Gery, a journey of about ten kilometers. No reason was found for Maurice to take them to Clermont, but it must have been for reasons of diversion. The village Thirimont is less than five kilometers from Solre Saint Gery, but perhaps going by way of Clermont was safer under the circumstances at the time.

They visited with Father Robert in Solre Saint Gery, then went to the home of Jean Dogne, another member of Group G. After three days of hiding with Dogne, they were then transported to the home of Mlle. Eugenie Lambert de Sivry in Bois de Martinsart, about five kilometers south of Solre Saint Gery, and a short distance from the French border to the west. They spent three weeks in the home of Lambert de Sivry, a teacher by profession and a member of the Comet Line.

On the night of May 1, they were visited by a doctor, a dentist, and another unknown man. They discussed the plans for the next move, and how it would be orchestrated. The doctor and dentist visited one more time to finalize the planned move, and told Don and Jim that they would be moved across the border and into Lille, France. At that point they would be met by other people in the French underground. They were assured that everything was in place and ready.

On the night of May 12, the unknown man who had accompanied the doctor and dentist on their first visit came to the home of Lambert de Sivry. The three left on foot, and traveled through the night, across the French border, and arrived at a farm house just before daylight. Around 8:00 a.m., two men that they did not know arrived by car to take them to Lille. By 11:00 a.m., they had arrived in Lille, and spent the day hiding in a doctor's office. About 5:00 p.m., a young man in his late twenties with a woman who was a few years younger arrived to get them. As it was discovered later, the couple were Dr. Leon Baron and his wife Edie, but they had not introduced themselves to the two airmen at the time that they met.

After an uneventful trip into the outskirts of Lille with the Barons, they soon came to a German police roadblock. No time was wasted by the Germans, and they immediately removed the two Americans from the car, then sent Dr. Baron and his wife down the road. It was very apparent to Don and Jim that they had been set up. The Barons had delivered them into the hands of the Germans. They had been betrayed by someone in the underground, either by Dr. Baron and his wife, or by someone in the Belgian underground who had been hiding them over the last three months. However it was done, and by whomever responsible, the results were the same. The hiding was over for Don and Jim. On May 13, 1944 their war was over, and their lives were about to change again.

In several conversations with Don over the years, he stated that he never understood why the French doctor and his wife delivered him and Jim into the hands of the Nazis, but he believed to his dying day that they were working with the enemy, not the French resistance movement.

chapter five

CAPTURE

After their capture at the roadblock, Jim and Don were soon separated. It was not unusual for this to happen, both for interrogation purposes and also because Jim was a commissioned officer and Don was a sergeant. Typically, newly acquired prisoners were sent to an interrogation center as soon as possible after capture. During the early part of the war, there was basically one interrogation center (Dulag Luft) located at Oberursel, Germany, which was near Frankfurt. Prisoners could be kept at Dulag Luft up to thirty days according to the Geneva Convention, but most were only there three or four days at most. Prisoners were moved quickly to the Dulag Luft, and Don was in Oberursel by May 16, 1944. The Germans would have started putting together paperwork for notifying the International Red Cross regarding his capture. They in turn would send notification to the Army Air Force, who would notify his family back home. This process was actually a high priority, but things happened much slower in 1944 than today. It would take awhile before the Allies would be notified.

It may be surprising to the reader that the enemy would move so quickly to inform the families and government of their opposing force about the welfare of the captured personnel. This was partially because the Geneva Convention spelled out the procedures that combatants were supposed to follow. But a large part of it was that the Germans, in this case, had prisoners who were being held by the United States, and they wished them to be treated fairly. The thinking was that if the American prisoners were treated fairly, then the German prisoners would be treated with fairness also. In speaking to the average person today about this, they often find this surprising. I feel that part of the bias comes from seeing old war movies in which the prisoners are tortured to gain information or as a form of punishment. Although this undoubtedly happened occasionally, it was not the rule, but rather the exception. Another reason for being surprised at fair treatment by the Germans could be because the treatment of Americans in the hands of the Japanese was often substandard and terrible. The same was true of American prisoners of the North Vietnamese during the Vietnam War. By and large, the treatment of American prisoners held by the Germans was much better than the treatment of either of the other countries named above. If comparing the treatment of German POWs held in the United States with American POWs held in Germany, it can certainly be seen that the Germans in the United States were treated better. A major part of the reason was that our physical country was not under attack, our supply lines were open, and there was access to better medical care and food.

It must be remembered we were waging an air war over the actual area where our captured airmen were being held. This fact will be revisited several times in the remainder of this work: the success of the Allied bombing campaign was denying the enemy of transportation, food, fuel, and the necessities of normal life. It was slowly strangling the German ability to live and fight, and the objective was to force them to surrender or to be decisively defeated. The fact that our captured soldiers, airmen, and sailors were living in German territory was an obstacle that we endeavored to avoid, but war is never fair or humane.

The reader will have to remember that not all Allied prisoners were tortured or treated unfairly, nor was life in a POW camp similar to a stay at a resort, either. It can be safely said that life in a POW camp was a mixture of boredom, extreme emotion, fear, and the constant wonder about what was going on in the "real world" outside the barbed wire enclosure. But all of that would come later. At this point, in Dulag Luft, Don and Jim were going through the first days of orientation in the experience of being a Prisoner of War.

The Germans were realistic enough to know that most crewmen flying missions over their occupied lands held no deep secrets about the

Allied war machine. During the interrogation, they sought information that they did not already know, but they seldom discovered anything new. Hundreds of airmen had been captured, and the Germans had learned about where they flew from, how the different models of aircraft performed, how big the bomb loads were, etc., but the big Allied plan for the war against them was even more obvious: bomb them in order to soften them up for a big land invasion, then push them back across western Europe while the Russian army pushed them back from eastern Europe. The big squeeze would eventually strangle them into defeat.

There was no secret about any of that. So, the Germans interrogated the new prisoners, looked for anything that they didn't already know, then sent them on to a prison. The biggest thing in the German's favor at the Dulag Luft was that the new prisoners were scared to death. They had no idea what was waiting for them. The Germans put the prisoners in a solitary room for awhile, then questioned them. Instead of threatening them, they found that it was more productive to put them at ease. Many Allied prisoners were surprised that more often than not the interrogators spoke perfect English. Many had lived for awhile in the United States, going to school or living for a time with relatives.

One prisoner discovered that the German officer questioning him spoke with a distinct accent from the south side of Chicago. He had spent a big part of his youth living with an aunt and uncle in Chicago before the family had to go back to Germany prior to the war. At another POW camp, a prisoner was recognized by one of the guards, an older man who had operated a butcher shop in New York City. He addressed the new young prisoner by name and asked how his family was doing. War is not only unfair and inhumane, but it can also be found to contain episodes of the surreal.

Don once told me of an experience that he had just after arriving at the Dulag Luft. Like all of the new prisoners, he was scared and on edge, not knowing what would happen next. He was all alone, and thousands of miles from home and anything familiar. He and several other prisoners were herded into an area enclosed with barbed wire like animals into a corral. As he was lost in the despair of his bad fortune, another prisoner wearing 2nd lieutenant bars excitedly came up to him and said, "Hey, aren't you Don Dinwiddie from Higbee? Do you remember me? I'm

Buddy Shaw from Fayette! I remember playing basketball against you in high school a couple of years ago!" Don said that life suddenly became bearable again after meeting up with a fellow Missourian in that strange and scary place, and for awhile, his loneliness disappeared. It must have felt the same for Robert "Buddy" Shaw as well, the navigator on a B-24. He'd jumped from the burning plane just seconds before it exploded, and was one of four who survived out of the crew of ten. Buddy was taken prisoner immediately upon landing in a field full of Germans in Belgium and had no hope of evasion. He was only at the Dulag Luft for a few days, then was sent to Stalag Luft III for the rest of the war. In researching information for this book, I was able to contact Lt. Shaw's son, Dr. Robert Shaw, Jr., in southwest Missouri. He shared stories of his father's war experiences, and told me that his dad was able to take a piece of barbed wire from Stalag Luft III when he was liberated.

Within a few days at Dulag Luft, Don was transferred to Stalag Luft IV. A "stalag", in loose translation, was a prison camp. "Luft" referred to air. Thus, Stalag Luft IV was "Air Prison Camp #4". The Germans usually put the commissioned officers in different locations than the noncommissioned. Jim Fowler was transferred to Stalag Luft I, a camp mostly for officers near the Baltic Sea in northern Germany. Stalag Luft IV, where Don was sent, was in Gross Tychow, Poland, and was one of the POW camps that was located furthest east in German-occupied territory. The commissioned/non-commissioned segregation policy was not always followed, for whatever reason. In a letter from Jim Fowler to Barney Rawlings after the latter had made it back to the States, Fowler related that "he saw Ferguson nearly every day". For some reason, non-com Ferguson was placed in a Stalag mainly used to house commissioned officers.

After the D-Day invasion of France on June 6, 1944, there was a great increase in Allied soldiers becoming prisoners, so the Germans had to change their operations and methods due to the influx. Also, a contributing factor was the transportation of prisoners from point of capture to transit centers and then to permanent Stalags. As Allied forces moved further into German-occupied areas, transportation was disrupted, and the Germans had to make do with what they had available. Likewise, after D-Day, the Dulag Luft that was at Oberursel wasn't able to handle the great number of prisoners, so other facilities had to be opened. As with the commissioned vs. noncommissioned segregation in different camps, the influx of prisoners after D-Day forced the Germans into placing some of the new prisoners from the Allied ground forces in the Stalags originally assigned to air force prisoners. The number of Allied prisoners increased greatly after the Battle of the Bulge from mid-December 1944 to late January 1945, placing a further burden on the Germans regarding the placement of prisoners.

When Don arrived at Stalag Luft IV, it had actually just opened, and he was one of the first prisoners. It was set up like most of the Stalags, with several buildings housing prisoners arranged in the middle of a large wire-enclosed area. There were certain wired off areas that were "warning" areas, then there were other areas after those that were "shoot-to-kill areas". The prisoners were informed that the warning area was not to be crossed without permission. Entering the warning area might be allowed to retrieve a stray soccer ball, etc., but not for traveling to another part of the camp. If one crossed the warning area without permission, they would be verbally commanded by the guards watching from the towers to exit the warning area and return to the area from which they had come. If a prisoner continued through the warning area and into the off-limits area, the guards had the authority to shoot to kill the transgressor. By the same token, any prisoner blatantly attempting to escape could be shot. This didn't happen often, but it *did* occur.

Escaping prisoners were not common. In spite of the common Allied order that "the duty of every prisoner is to escape", the reality of this had to be tempered with the realization that if one did escape from a Stalag deep in German territory, one had no place to go. A downed airman parachuting out over Belgium or France could count on a good chance of being aided by the underground, but the German citizenry was not overly friendly to those who had been bombing them night and day for the previous three or four years.

Another deterrent to escaping was that the physical condition of many of the prisoners was such that they didn't have the stamina to attempt an escape.

The lack of nutritious food was the biggest complaint of the prisoners, and it was sometimes stated that it was thought that the

Germans were purposely starving prisoners in order to make them more docile and unable to make a run for it. While this might have been a benefit for the German captors, they were also experiencing the same lack of food.

Having asked Don about his treatment by the Germans while he was in captivity, he said that it was "better than I would've expected". I think that the fear of the unknown made the fear of the POW camps worse. Nobody in their right mind would want to be taken captive by the enemy that that they had been bombing. But the truth of the matter is that most of the men had been expecting worse, just like Don. The fact that they didn't get tortured or beaten or stood up against a wall and shot was a pleasant alternative to what was conjured up in their minds. To get an accurate assessment of how the Americans were treated, one must remember certain important factors. First, we had been bombing the Germans for almost two years when the Fowler crew was shot down. By the time of the Frankfurt mission, the Germans were definitely feeling the effects of that bombing campaign. With the British bombing at night and the Americans bombing during the day, the Germans were under a continuous attack from the air. Much of the infrastructure of the occupied territories was destroyed and had to be rebuilt. Many of the factories and refineries used by the enemy were rendered useless for periods of time. As was seen by the Germans scavenging the *G.I. Sheets* for the unused fuel, they were in the middle of a fuel crisis. And all of these setbacks for the German war machine were brought about by the air war, because the ground offensive didn't begin until June 6, 1944. And although the Americans tried to bomb strategic targets affecting the German military, and to avoid the indiscriminate bombing of civilians, the effects of the bombing certainly spilled over into the everyday lives of the German population. Especially brutal to the civilian population was the night bombing of the British, which was not aimed at strategic military targets. The bombing also affected the lives of the POWs held in the Stalags. The availability and delivery of food and mail was disrupted and noticed by the prisoners. Don often told me that the German guards complained as much about the lack of food as the prisoners themselves did.

POWs could send and receive mail, but it was slow, and it was strictly censored. When stopping to remember that the mail had to travel in and out of a war zone, across the Atlantic Ocean, and across the United States, it seems a miracle that any correspondence was ever delivered.

Usually the mail consisted of a short "Kriegie Card", a post card-sized letter named after the nickname the prisoners had given themselves, a shortened version of the German word for "prisoner of war", *kriegesgefanengen.* Kriegies were also able to receive packages sent from the U.S., but after both the Allied and German censors inspected the parcels en route, the contents were often partially or completely missing or damaged. The International Red Cross also saw to it that the POWs received parcels containing toiletries, cigarettes, and candy as well as recreational materials such as sports equipment and books. As with the packages from home, often these materials were delivered with missing contents, if they arrived at all.

Aside from the lack of food and the poor conditions, the biggest problem for the prisoners was boredom. The POWs tried to organize activities to pass the time, such as soccer and baseball, card tournaments, and even organizing and performing plays. The POW leaders tried to maintain military discipline and structured physical activities to keep the men in the best physical condition as possible in spite of the lack of proper rations. Above all, the men needed to be reminded of the fact that the war would one day be over, and that they would be going home. How did they know this? There were signs....

One thing was very obvious: there were fewer and fewer German planes in the sky. There would be the sounds and sights of large formations of Allied bombers flying overhead, seemingly unbothered by German fighters. New prisoners coming into the camps were the best source of news, and they had plenty. The newbies told them of the huge Allied invasion of Normandy on June 6, 1944. It was the largest invasion that had ever taken place in the history of warfare. Thousands of American, British, Canadian, and Free French soldiers came ashore on the beaches of Normandy in several waves. While it was deadly to the first men ashore, the mass of Allied men couldn't be held back, and the Germans were soon being pushed back across France and Belgium to the east. For the first time, there were ground forces in Europe, and the

Germans, already weakened by the years of aerial bombing were on the run. The war couldn't last much longer.

Another thing, strictly *verbotten* on the part of the staff of the Stalag, was the lack of morale and the rumors going around through the ranks of the guards. Much of the guard and prison staff was made up by those men who were too old or previously wounded and not fit for combat. Many of these men were sick of the war, sick of Hitler's policies, and seemed to know that the war was hopeless. Some seemed to identify more with their prisoners than their own army. Some, unfortunately, seemed to become more bitter and mean. It was obvious to the prisoners that there seemed to be something very different as time passed after the D-Day invasion.

In reference to the guards and prison staff, it must be noted that one must always remember that there was a huge difference in the Adolph Hitler of 1944 and the man that rose to power in the early 1930s. Hitler was a very charismatic leader and orator who won the trust of the German populace as the man who would bring them out of the economic ruin they had been suffering since their defeat in WWI. His plans to not only revive Germany but make it a leader on the world stage won over the hearts of the citizens, and many of them believed that Germany could dominate the industrial and economic world. Unfortunately, Hitler and his Nazi fanatics believed in total world domination. Within Europe, the dirty secret of Hitler's plan to rid the world of inferior ethnic groups and to engineer the rise of the Aryan race was being seen by the systematic killing of European Jews. Some of Hitler's own generals were seeing the problem, and some had tried to assassinate him in July of 1944. Unfortunately, the attempt failed, as had the previous five attempts, and Hitler seemed to be more erratic in behavior after that. The only true believers in Hitler were those who were as crazy as he was.

By the end of 1944, only the fanatics and the dreamers felt that Germany had a chance at winning the war. The advancing Allied forces from France and Belgium in the west toward Germany in the east had been quicker than planned. This, however, had left the leading edge of the advancing forces rather thin. Hitler, in a last ditch plan to quickly attack the Allies and force them to retreat or surrender, undertook what Americans called The Battle of the Bulge. The "bulge" was the Allied battle line that was pushed back in eastern Belgium and northeastern

France when the Germans made a surprise attack in that area, stalling the U.S. forces near the town of Bastogne.

The Germans were lucky because the weather was so bad that the Allied air forces couldn't fly. After the weather cleared, however, the air superiority of the Allies enabled them to attack German positions and drop supplies to the stranded Allied ground troops. The Battle of the Bulge lasted for almost six bloody weeks before the battle lines were restored back to the original point, and the Germans were pushed back.

This six-week battle was the longest and bloodiest of the entire war for the Allies, and the third worst in history. Hitler's plan was to encircle the Allies and capture the port city of Antwerp, cutting their supply lines. If this could be accomplished, Hitler felt that the British and the Americans would have sought a peace settlement with Germany, leaving him to fight with the Russians advancing from the east. In spite of Allied losses during this campaign, the effect on the fate of Germany was more devastating. The German situation was made more dire by their losses, and the fact that the Allied drive toward Germany was back in full swing. With the exception of small skirmishes, there was no further German offensive moves during the rest of the war. Hitler's dreams may have continued, but his generals knew that the war had grown shorter for all of them. The Germans had captured many Allied prisoners during the Battle of the Bulge, and the new prisoners coming into the camps brought the news of the recent German offensive, and that the Allies were still on the move despite this setback. It gave the POWs more hope that the war would soon be ending.

chapter six

DEATH MARCH

As the Americans and British were slowly moving eastward toward Germany, the Russian forces were moving west toward Germany from the east. Germany was obviously being squeezed from both sides, and there was a definite unease by the Germans regarding the Russian advance. With the German invasion of Russia on the Eastern Front earlier in the war, the Russians had lost an astonishing 20,000,000 people (civilians and military) to the Germans, and they were looking forward to invading Germany and seeking retribution.

One night in late January 1945, just after the Allied forces had regained the territory that it had lost due to the German invasion in the Battle of the Bulge, the POWs at Stalag Luft IV could see the flash of artillery to the east. Since Stalag Luft IV was at the far east of the German territory, and based on the news that had come in with the new prisoners, the guns could only be those of the Russian army. This gave hope to the prisoners that maybe they would be liberated soon. It meant a lot more to the Germans. Their fear of the approaching Russians could lead to the POWs being relocated. According to what Don had related to his daughter Kim in later years, a rumor had started circulating that the camp was going to be evacuated. In trying to prepare for a possible march to another location, Don started walking as much as possible within the confines of Stalag Luft IV to get himself in shape. Hopefully, some of his fellow POWs had followed his example.

An order came down from the German high command to evacuate the sick and wounded prisoners by train. A few days later more POWs were transported out of the camp. All of them were westbound, but to where? Nobody seemed to have a clear idea about what was going on. Even the guards and camp personnel were mystified, but the word was going around that the Germans were trying to avoid having to fight or surrender to the Russians. The POWs were afraid that they were being taken away to be executed, or to be held at some secret location as hostages by the Germans in order to demand concessions from the Allies. After the war was over, the German general who was over all of the prisoner of war camps testified that there were secret contingency plans drawn up shortly after the Normandy invasion in June of 1944 that actually considered both of those possibilities. Hitler had considered holding the POWs hostage to demand American and British concessions if Germany had to surrender.

Lieutenant General Gottlob Berger, who was in charge of all the prison camps during 1944, said that although these ideas had been set forth, the real reason that the prisoners were moved west was because of the 1929 Geneva Convention. It was ruled in that agreement that prisoners of war must not be in a potential combat zone, and the rapid movement of the Russian Army was putting Stalag Luft IV in danger. General Berger stated that all of the prisoners were to be moved by train, but the sudden close proximity of the Russians made it impossible to arrange the necessary rail travel, so only the sick and wounded were moved in that manner. All the others were forced to walk west during the bitter German winter.

While in no way does it excuse the German high command for moving the prisoners in such a manner, the breakdown in communication and command structure in the German military and government was certainly a contributing factor as to why it happened. The Geneva Convention notwithstanding, nobody in the German military wanted to be caught in the Russian advance. Short of deserting their posts and abandoning the prisoners, there wasn't much the German guards could do but try to fight the Russians or surrender. To do either would have been certain death for the German guards and prison camp staff, and probably the same fate for many of the prisoners. Additionally, most of the guards and staff were very old, very young, or physically unable to serve in combat, so they would have been virtually useless in battle. In their westward advance toward Germany, the Russians had demonstrated their brutality and disregard for any human life in their path, and an untrained force would have had no chance to slow or stop them.

Berger was indicted by the Allied War Crimes Tribunal in 1947 for the deaths of those in the march, but he was acquitted because he was found correct in his explanation of how the march came about. He was convicted in another trial in 1949 for being complicit in the deaths of European Jews, and was sentenced to twenty-five years in prison for his role in that. While the pitiful excuse "I was just following orders" is not a valid reason for his role in the move of the prisoners, Berger could do nothing to fix the situation at hand. If anything, the Germans should have ordered the prisoners to be moved months before.

Whatever the reasons for why it happened, on February 6, 1945 the order came to evacuate the remainder of the POWs from Stalag Luft IV. In groups of 250 to 300 men, an estimated 6,000 prisoners remaining in the camp were told that they would be departing in a few hours.

They were informed that they would be marching, and that they would be on the move for about three days. They were not told what the destination was, or how far away it was, but that they would be travelling west. Inwardly, the fact that they were heading toward the advancing American and British forces probably motivated many of the prisoners. Despite having been suffering from lack of nutrition and good medical care, all of the men were young and in relatively good shape, so most of them felt that three days would be no trouble. The camp leaders told the POWs that they could take whatever they felt they could carry, and also made a shipment of Red Cross food packages available to them. Within a few hours of being told of their departure, the men of Stalag Luft IV left Gross Tychow, Poland for some unknown western destination.

February is one of the coldest months in Europe at the latitude where the prisoners were located. The snow was deep, and most of the men had insufficient footwear. They were told that the march would be for three days, and if it had only been that long, it would've been difficult, but doable. Little did they know that the advertised three days would evolve into a trip of over thirty times that long. The forced march became known by the terms "The Long March", "The Stalag Death March", "The Death March", or simply, "The March". Sadly, this event has been largely ignored by historians of WWII, but has been well documented in the German files as well as the anecdotal records of the prisoners who were there.

When most people hear the term “Death March” in reference to WWII, what comes to mind is the infamous Bataan Death March that took place in the Philippines. During that forced march at the hands of the Japanese, approximately 75,000 American and Filipino prisoners covered about eighty-five miles in six days, with thousands dying at the hands of their captors. By the time the German Death March had ended, the prisoners had travelled over 600 miles, roughly the distance from Chicago to Topeka. They had marched eighty-six days, and it was estimated that 1,300 men perished. Not only were the men from Stalag Luft IV on the move, but also POWs from other camps in the eastern German-occupied territory. Any camp threatened by the Russian advance was evacuated. The German “Death March” was named thus because of the brutal weather, lack of rations, and the distance covered, not because of the brutality of the guards. Poor logistical planning and appropriate preparations were certainly lacking and the fault of the German high command. It is a fact that some of the prisoners were mistreated and died at the hands of their guards, but again, that was the exception.

When the men left Stalag Luft IV, they expected a three-day trip. Many of them had brought blankets, packs, and, of course, the Red Cross food packages. After several hours of trudging through the deep snow, many of them tossed aside the some of their load. If they were only moving for three days, many of them decided they could do without the burden. This was a huge mistake. One report stated that the only rations that the Germans supplied on the march was a cup of thin soup at mid-day and two potatoes and two pieces of bread at the end of the day.

Since the German guards weren’t eating much more, if any, than the prisoners, that seems to be an indication that they were not properly informed of route, times, and destination. If they knew that they would be on the road for three months, why would they have allowed the extra rations be thrown to the side of the road? It’s an indication that the Germans on the march were as misinformed as the prisoners.

As the march continued, the prisoners foraged for their own food. If they passed a farm that had root crops still in the ground, they dug them up. If they could catch a chicken, they made a meal out of it. By the end of the forced march, they were eating cats, dogs, rats—anything that would sustain them. As the weather warmed, they ate wild onions and other natural food plants. Don didn't talk much about the march, but he did say that his small stature resulted in him being the scavenger of root cellars along the route. If they passed a farm that looked promising, they would check for root cellars holding potatoes, turnips, anything edible. If they found something, he would be lowered into the hole to see what it held. The job did have its perks. If he found something, he got the first bite.

Again, the guards were starting to identify with the prisoners. They were all on the road to some unknown destination with little food, and they all worked together to keep themselves moving and fed as well as possible. The guards did keep some semblance of order, and their presence allowed them to find churches, factories, barns, etc, in which to spend the night. They also kept angry civilians away from the prisoners. As they went by some German civilians, some threw rocks at the prisoners, and yelled at them. But they also passed some who gave them food and water. And truth be known, it was the same with the guards. Some were friendly, some were barbaric. There were instances of guards dragging a sick prisoner into the woods and coming back alone. But there were also guards who shared their supplies and rations with the prisoners, as well.

It must be remembered that much of the German populace had become disenchanted with Hitler and his minions as the war progressed, and by late winter of 1945, it was no wonder that some of the guards on the march felt more in common with their charges than with the German military leadership.

The water supply had dwindled early in the march, and the men were forced to drink from roadside ditches to slake their thirst. This brought on widespread dysentery and other bowel problems. Some of the guards found a wagon that allowed some of the sickest men to take turns riding and resting, but it had to be pulled by some of their more able buddies. It was just as well that there were no horses…they would've probably been eaten anyway.

At the end of a day's travel, the distance covered would vary depending upon the weather and the road conditions. Reportedly, the shortest distance covered in one day was five kilometers, and the longest was thirty kilometers. The only way that the men could judge the distance was by the markings found on the German roads. They knew that the "three days march" had been wrong, whether intentionally or not. The bottom line seemed to be that the days, however many, would be spent in marching, and the nights would be spent sleeping in whatever location they could find at the end of the day. They tried to find shelter wherever they could, but sometimes they had to sleep in open fields. The days of marching and the lack of food and rest were taking their toll on the men, but reportedly the morale was good. As the days dragged on, they started seeing groups of German civilians on the roads, also travelling westward away from the Russians advancing from the east.

Besides the question of how long they would be marching, another large unknown was their destination. After several days of marching on the twisting, turning roads, most men lost whatever sense of direction that they had, and without a good knowledge of the geography, nobody knew where they were, much less where they could be going. The guards probably knew where they were, but they claimed that they had no idea what the destination was. One thing that did leak out was that supposedly all POWs from all of the Stalags close to the Russian advance were on the march. They were strung out over several routes in groups similar to those that had left Stalag Luft IV, and all were headed toward the west, toward the American and British lines.

In speaking with Don about this, he said that was an unofficial bit of information that had spread through the group of men that he was with, but nobody saw any prisoners on the road from other camps. The information that Don was getting turned out to be true, and several thousand POWs were on the move toward the west, but he never encountered any of them.

In doing further research into this exodus of prisoners, I've discovered that there was definitely a destination in which they were trying to reach. The group from Stalag IV was headed toward Fallingbostel, a town located about sixty-five kilometers north of Hanover in north central Germany. Located there were two prison camps, Stalag XIb and Stalag 357. In late March they finally arrived at their destination, but found that the over-crowded camps had no accommodations for the extra prisoners.

They were able to crowd in and fend for themselves. Although food and bunks were scarce, at least they had stopped marching and were able to get showers and deloused. Incredibly, after being there only one week, they were once again put on the move.

And, as with the initial march, the guards seemed as perplexed as the POWs. Looking back in retrospect, it seemed as if the Germans had gotten word that the American and British forces were getting closer to them from the west. It became obvious that the German guards, and whoever commanded them, didn't want to meet the Russians, but they also were reluctant to run into the Americans. Those responsible for the prisoners were still German soldiers, no matter how badly the war was going for them, and they were reluctant to turn the POWs over to the Allied forces for fear of being labeled traitors by the Nazi government. Oddly enough, the Stalag IV prisoners were marched back toward the east, backtracking the same path that they had followed westward just a few weeks earlier. According to prisoner reports, they seemed to wander aimlessly in various directions from day to day, as if the Germans were stalling for time.

During this time of indeterminate wandering, an odd thing happened. As with the original march, the prisoners were sent on this second stint of marching in groups of a few hundred. Some of the groups woke up one morning to discover that their guards had disappeared. Don had shared a conversation with me in which he told me that this had happened to his group. He was with a group of other men who had found a barn in which to spend the night. When they woke up, they found nobody in charge, the guards having left. It was a frightening situation for the POWs.

As far as they knew, the war was still going on, and there had been no German surrender. The lack of guards didn't mean that they were free…it just meant that they were now a ragtag group of unarmed U.S. soldiers on the loose in enemy territory. Even though they were technically prisoners, they were still the enemy, and their missing guards were also their protection from angry civilians.

German soldiers and guards often had to intervene with mobs of angry civilians to protect downed airmen and POWs in past situations, and the Stalag Luft IV men were very aware of that. The big question was what they should do.

The consensus was that they should take their chances and return to walking toward the west. They had no idea of where the Allied lines were, but moving in that direction was the only option. They would probably face some civilians, and maybe they would be "recaptured" by a roving German military unit. They had been marching for the past three months in horrendous conditions, and as a group, the men that Don was with decided that they would head west and deal with whatever happened. They met several groups of civilians on the road, and those that they encountered seemed mystified to see the Allied men, but nothing happened other than an occasional dirty look or shouted curse.

Everyone seemed to feel that the war was grinding to a halt, and the Americans prisoners and the German civilians were tired of it. The POWs were allowed to travel unharmed. Don reported that some of the German civilians even shared their food with the Americans.

Not all of the abandoned prisoners marched west toward the Allied advance. Some stayed in one place, hoping that the advancing forces would eventually come to them. Unfortunately, they were rescued by the wrong Allies, the Russians. In keeping with their reputation for meaningless brutality and unpredictable behavior, they kept the POWs detained as prisoners of the Russian forces. It was several days before the Americans advanced to their position and were able to liberate the American POWs from the Russians, who were technically their allies.

In the absurdity of war, other bizarre stories leaked out. One group of prisoners, getting close to the advancing Americans, had the strange occurrence of having their German guards insist that the POWs take the German weapons and begged the prisoners to take them, their guards, as prisoners.

In another scenario, as a group of prisoners marched past a small German airfield, two of the POWs stole a plane and flew it to the Allied lines. A group of British POWs passed a field containing several horses, so they promptly jumped on them and rode like cavalry to the Allied lines. Even though the Germans had not surrendered, it was evident that the war was over for most practical purposes.

Don's situation was wasn't as dramatic as stealing a plane or riding to freedom on horseback, but it was somewhat unusual. On May 2, 1945, their group came upon a few German soldiers who apparently understood the futility of trying to recapture the unguarded prisoners. The Germans simply pointed down a particular road and told them to march in that direction. After walking along the road for a short distance, they heard a motorcycle coming toward them from around a curve. Soon a British soldier on the bike came into view. He stopped to tell them that if they were tired of wandering, they could follow him down the road and become the guests of the British 8th Army Royal Dragoons in the town of Gudow. After eighty-six days and 600 miles of walking, Don and his group of POWs from Stalag Luft IV were liberated. Although tired and sick, the former prisoners raucously rejoiced at joining up with the British. They were finally safe, and for all practical purposes, their war was over at that point.

Another bit of irony: Just a few days after the POWs were taken out of Stalag XI on their second meandering forced march back toward the east, Fallingbostel was taken by the Allies and became the first POW camp to be liberated. I'm sure that the POWs from Stalag Luft IV really didn't care at this point. They were enjoying the company of the Royal Dragoons.

In some official documents you will see that Don was liberated by the Russians. That did not happen. Some groups of prisoners from Stalag Luft IV were liberated by the Russians, but not Don's group. It was definitely the British that gave them their freedom.

chapter seven

HOMEWARD BOUND

Although there are different dates often given, the official unconditional surrender of the Germans came on May 8, 1945. For several weeks after that, there were still pockets of Nazi hold-outs who refused to honor the surrender, so the war continued in somewhat of a police action. For all practical purposes, the war had stopped, and the steady advance of Allied forces from Normandy to Germany that began on June 6 began to reverse itself. Slowly, troops began to be moved back toward the west after the fighting stopped, and camps that had been originally set up to move replacement soldiers to the front lines were now set up to reverse the flow. Not only were the fighting troops being pulled back, plans were implemented to deal with the thousands of POWs that had been liberated. Several of these camps had been given code names of American and British cigarette brands, mostly around the French ports of Le Havre and Marseilles. Camp Lucky Strike, Camp Chesterfield, and Camp Old Gold were the largest, vast tent cities housing over 60,000 POWs.

Some POWs had a difficult time when they suddenly found themselves back in the "real world". The long process of healing their wounds, whether physical or emotional, had begun. Don said that the first thing on the minds of most in his group when they met up with the British force was food. The Brits warned them to take it easy on the food because they weren't ready for it, but most of them over-indulged anyway. Don said he was sick from eating too much too quickly, but it was great food and impossible to ignore it. He said that at that point in his life, that was the best meal he had ever eaten. One of the most important things that was done immediately was that all of the rescued POWs were given a small postcard that they were to fill out. It would be mailed home to tell their next of kin that they were liberated from the Germans.

The process of recovery for the repatriated prisoners was basically a simple one: physical exams, medical treatment, food, and relaxation. They were also debriefed by military intelligence in order to find out information about what they knew about their fellow crew members. Don was moved to one of the Cigarette Camps shortly after he was liberated by the British. There he and all the other POWs were treated as the conquering heroes that they were. They were able to have real showers, real food, new uniforms, some back pay, and no duty. As they recovered, they were allowed some freedom of movement, and many of them obtained souvenirs of their war. German helmets, weapons, battle flags, uniform patches, etc, were everywhere.

After spending time in the Cigarette Camps, the POWs that could travel were soon bound for the United States. In Don's case, he came back on the *Queen Mary*, the same ship that had delivered the Fowler crew to the U.K. en route to Molesworth. Certainly, the trip home was more enjoyable than the trip to the war. For sure the ship didn't have to worry about U-boat attacks.

Most of the POWs went to convalescent hospitals for medical treatment for sickness and neglected wounds. They also were fed controlled diets to help mend their malnutrition. While in convalescent care, some of the former crew members sent letters to their friends. Barney Rawlings reported in his memoirs that he heard from Richard Arrington, Loren Zimmer, and Joe Thompson after they had been returned to the States in November 1944 after being liberated in September. He was interested in their stories, and glad that they had made it home. He had received a Kriegie letter from Jim Fowler from Stalag Luft I and knew the story about him and Don being captured. The last crew member unaccounted for was Curt Finley. In late November 1944, the Red Cross notified the family of Finley that he had been taken prisoner by the Germans in Southern France, just short of making it over the mountains into Spain.

Don was sent to a convalescent center in San Antonio, Texas after coming back to the United States. He was officially honorably discharged from the U.S. Army Air Force on October 28, 1945.

Just a few days after Don's passing in 2005, Grandma Jean asked me and my brother-in-law Jack to go to the basement storage area and find a box that Don had sealed and put away, not to be opened. She said that it was time to reveal its contents.

When we cut the tape sealing the box and opened it, we found a cleaned and folded Army Air Force uniform shirt and cap, apparently the ones that he had last worn when he was mustered out of the service. There were also souvenirs and trinkets from the war, obviously picked up before leaving Europe after his liberation. There was nothing dramatic, just stuff found in old trunks like countless other veterans had left behind in the wake of their passing. There was a small Nazi swastika flag, some German uniform insignia, a belt buckle, and some spent bullets. Why had he kept them hidden?

These were memories that never lost their raw edges, from times that he didn't want to remember, but at the same time they were from the most important time in his life. This was a common problem of the fighting man, trying to forget about almost dying in combat with your comrades, but never wanting to forget it as being the most intense time of your life.

It would always be a memory of a defining moment in life, but it wasn't a memory that you wanted to revisit often. Better to box it up until a better time. Don's daughter Kim stated that she had a childhood memory of her dad getting out the box on occasion, looking at the contents, then sealing it up and putting it away. Although Don did open up to me about several aspects of their last mission and his time of evasion and capture, it was obvious that, like most veterans who had experienced real combat, he would never find that "better time" to be comfortable with his box of memories.

On that winter day of January 29, 1944, after the *G.I. Sheets* slid to a stop on its belly in the muddy field on the hill at the edge of Solre Saint Gery, the crew scattered and went into hiding. Some of them never again saw any of their crew mates after those last hectic and frightening minutes as they were being tended to by total strangers from the village.

In several separate situations in the last few hours, they had all been near death. They had been shot at by the enemy and wounded. They had seen the blood from themselves and their fellow crew members. They had seen one of their group killed. They had been inside their aircraft almost five miles above the earth as it was being destroyed not only by enemy bullets but by its own failing engines.

Then suddenly they were set upon by two enemy fighter planes, and were totally helpless to whatever they dished out, but miraculously they were allowed to land their doomed bomber on that muddy field in Belgium. Individually and collectively, their lives had drastically changed during the five hours after they had departed Molesworth on their way to Frankfurt.

chapter eight

AFTER THE WAR

After the last mission of the *G.I. Sheets*, the crew went their separate ways that day at Marly's Field in Belgium. Each had their own personal adventure that would probably serve as the defining moment in their life and would forever be etched in their memory. The problem was, did they want to remember it? As with many veterans of traumatic experiences, how they dealt with it was their decision. As Barney Rawlings told me, and as he wrote in his recollections, nobody really wanted to talk about that last mission and its aftermath until many years later. He had communicated with Curtis Finley through letters, but he said that Finley gave him the impression that he didn't want to talk about the experience or the war, and never explained what had happened to him after they had parted company in that patch of woods the evening of the crash. Rawlings said that at that point he also decided to leave the war behind him, and simply enjoyed his life as an airline pilot for TWA, becoming a captain flying international routes. He passed away in 2004 at the age of 84.

Like Rawlings, all of the surviving crew members except Jim Fowler went back into civilian life to pursue their own endeavors. Fowler stayed in the Air Force and later retired as a colonel, having at one point in his career been in command of a U.S. Air Force base in France before his retirement in 1972. He died in 1997 at the age of 76.

Navigator Joseph Thompson, along with Loren Zimmer and Richard Arrington, was liberated by U.S. Army forces in Belgium in September 1944. Thompson went back to being a barber in Texas, and later became involved in local politics. He was unfortunately killed in a traffic accident in 1949. He was thirty-four years old.

Ball turret gunner Richard Arrington went back home to New Orleans after returning stateside. He died of natural causes in 1973 at the age of fifty-three.

Engineer Curtis Finley died in 1980 in Spokane, Washington at the age of sixty-six and is buried at Schuyler, Nebraska, where he was born.

Loren Zimmer, the only man to have bailed out of the damaged *G.I. Sheets*, retired in California after thirty-one years in the aerospace industry with the McDonnell-Douglas company. He passed away in 2001 at the age of eighty.

Bombardier Alvin Taylor returned to the United States and worked as an aeronautical engineer on aircraft and space vehicles with NASA. He died in Colorado at age ninety-four in 2015, the last living member of the Fowler crew.

Jack Ferguson, who was the replacement tail gunner for the original crew member Harry Wallrobenstein, never saw himself as a regular member of the crew. True to that status, not much is available about Ferguson post-war. His available military records show errors and aren't reliable if one searches under his name and military serial number. There was little to no contact between him and other crew after the war, but he did reach out to Barney Rawlings shortly after his return to the States to tell him that he was still plagued with problems from his wounds on the last mission, but he was happy to have survived. He also stated that he had been in the same POW camp (Stalag Luft I) as Jim Fowler and Al Taylor, which had been a comfort.

Wallrobenstein had a story that didn't reveal itself until sometime many years after the war. Nobody had seen him after the incident in which a flak round had narrowly missed blowing his head off in the tail gun position. After telling Don Dinwiddie that he thought the Germans were actually trying to kill him, he wasn't seen again. Late one night in the early 1970s, nearly thirty years after the incident, Don got a phone call from a noisy bar. The man on the line was obviously drunk, and after he'd babbled for a bit, Don figured out that it was Harry Wallrobenstein. Harry was crying, and apologetic. He told Don that he was sorry for letting down the rest of the crew by his disappearance. Obviously scared at the time, Wallrobenstein had gone AWOL (Absent Without Leave) rather than fly in combat again. Don assured him that it was understandable, and Harry hung up the phone, never to be heard from again. Wallrobenstein probably had to serve some time in the stockade for his disappearance and was in all likelihood assigned to another job other than flying. In checking the records of the 303rd Bomb Group, I was pleasantly surprised to see that he was back on flight status after a few months and flew fourteen missions as a gunner. I would like to think that knowing of the disappearance of his old crew gave him the courage to try again to do what he'd been trained to do. Harry died Sept 29, 1975 in Pittsburgh. He was sixty-two-years-old.

Miller Jackson, the only member of the crew that was killed in action, was officially pronounced dead after being taken to a hospital after the crash. According to most of the crew members and Dr. Verstraeten, he had actually died at the scene. His body was buried in a local cemetery in Belgium, then it was later moved to the American Cemetery in Liege. After the war, his body was taken to Arlington National Cemetery near Washington, D.C. He was once the "old man" of the crew, but now remains the youngest, forever at age thirty-eight-years-old.

Don Dinwiddie, the youngest of the crew on the day of the Frankfurt mission at twenty-years-old, returned home to Higbee, Missouri after the war. He and his brother, Archie Jr, attended Central Methodist College in nearby Fayette. In 1950, he married Miss Irma Jean Amick of Glasgow, Missouri. Don held several jobs in construction and manufacturing before being offered a job in the Disability Determinations branch of the Missouri Department of Elementary and Secondary Education. The job that he took required him to move to Cape Girardeau, Missouri, so in 1961 Don and Jean and their daughters Donna and Kim moved to Cape. He eventually became a supervisor in his office, retiring in 1985.

I met Don in 1988, and we chatted about his experience in the war. He didn't tell me much that was in-depth, other than he was a radio operator, was shot down, was a POW, and made it back home. Over the later years, he told me more. I didn't probe, and only took what he offered. I know that he had been thoroughly disgusted by the fact that he and Jim Fowler had been betrayed by the French doctor and his wife for delivering them to the Germans at the roadblock outside of Lille.

After his retirement, Don enjoyed fishing for trout and crappie. He and Jean bought a camper trailer and often went to Bennett Springs and Horseshoe Lake to stay a few days and connect with his brothers or go with some of his fishing buddies from church. The war seemed to be the last thing on his mind as he fished and camped and doted on his grandchildren, but I'm sure that it was always there in the dark corners of his memory. He always played down his role in winning the war, and when asked about what he had done in the war, he would always finish by saying, "But I was just one of many who took part in the war. Just one of many…."

But that's exactly what it had taken to defeat the Japanese and Germans in WWII, many like him. And like the others, he was just one of many who answered the call to duty, volunteering for a dangerous job that nobody had ever experienced before. He and other young men went off in terrible conditions to fly hundreds of miles and drop bombs on the Germans who had overrun most of Europe. For over two years the British and Americans fought the Germans from the air, hoping to drive them to their knees so that the ground invasion would work. After the invasion of Normandy on June 6, 1944, Allied ground troops fought a bloody battle to push the Germans out of France, Belgium, and Holland. Much of the fighting was brutal and unthinkable, but the stake was driven through the heart of the German war machine less than a year after D-Day. It would not have been possible without the thousands of young men in their bombers.

As the decades passed after the war, talking about their experiences came a little easier. I know that Don would often tell me about a little thing now and then, as if it had just reappeared in his memory. He told me about a mission in which it was extremely cold. He said that he thought that the outside air temperature gauge in his radio compartment had failed because it was indicating such a low temperature. He checked with the reading that the pilots had, and it checked out... it really *was* that cold. He told me that he was happy that he had a heated "office" in which to work. Another time he told me about how terribly the Russian prisoners were treated in Stalag Luft IV. He said that the

Americans weren't mistreated (except for the common complaints about food and mail), but that the Russians, in their separate compound, were intentionally treated cruelly.

One notable thing that Don related to me was about returning home from a mission to Germany. The formation didn't have a fighter escort all the way to the target and back, but as they were headed back to Molesworth, they were met by P-51s of the 332nd Fighter Group. The fighters had their tails painted red and were easy to identify. Their nickname was the "Redtails", but they were more officially known as the "Tuskegee Airmen". The unit was made up of all African-American pilots, and they were highly respected. They never lost a bomber that they were escorting. Don had nothing but admiration for them, for how aggressively they flew, and for what they had to overcome to do their duty. He said that the bomber crews always felt well-protected when the Redtails were with them.

Barney Rawlings was also finding the war easier to discuss. Al Taylor, living in Texas, reached out to Barney and told him about a reunion of the 303rd Bomb Group that was going to be held in 1986 in the Dallas/Ft. Worth area. They decided to get in touch with any of the old crew that they could locate. They both were excited with the possibility of seeing their old comrades

By that time, Arrington, Ferguson, and Finley had passed away from natural causes, and Thompson had been killed in the car accident. But Don Dinwiddie, Loren Zimmer, and Jim Fowler were all located and united with Al Taylor and Barney Rawlings in Ft. Worth. It was the first time in forty-two years that they were able to meet face-to-face. The last time that they had been together they had been scared kids in a muddy farm field in Belgium.

A short time after the Ft. Worth reunion, Barney was on a layover on a TWA flight in Belgium. As a pilot flying international flights, he often found himself flying over some of the same areas that he had overflown on missions during the war. He decided that he would go to Solre Saint Gery to visit the site of their crash landing.

As he walked over Marly's Field, the same muddy farm ground that he'd last been in 1944, he was guided by some of the local residents. There were still small pieces of aluminum left here and there from the

G.I. Sheets, remains of the German salvage operation that scavenged the plane. As the memories came flooding back, he felt emotion overwhelming him and tears came. He felt a hand on his shoulder, and a man's voice saying, "Yes, Barney, this is a sad place...." The voice belonged to Arthur Derenne, the fourteen year-old in 1944, who had quickly arrived at the crash site that day and urged Barney and Curt Finley to run to the woods to avoid the Germans.

Rawlings wasn't the only one who was moved by the old memories and the recollections of that day in 1944. Several of the local residents of Soule Saint Gery during 1944 still lived there and were still feeling the emotions of that time. Through the efforts of Arthur Derenne, plans were made to design and build a monument to the Fowler crew specifically, and in general to all of the Americans who fought the war to rid Belgium of the Nazi invaders.

As the monument was nearing completion, plans were made to have a ceremony to dedicate it, and all the surviving members of the Fowler crew were invited to attend as guest of honor. In the summer of 1987, Jim Fowler, Barney Rawlings, Don Dinwiddie, Loren Zimmer, along with their wives, and the widow and son of Curtis Finley made the trip to Belgium to attend the celebration.

They were able to reconnect with many of the people who had rescued, hidden, and cared for them forty-three years earlier. It was a time for giving thanks and reliving what had happened to each of them during the war.

Not only did the citizens of Solre Saint Gery take part, but the Belgian Air Force arranged for a speaker to thank the Americans for their service, and also had a flight of F-16s perform a tribute flyover. Ironically, they came from the same base at Florennes at which the Focke Wulf FW-190s were based that shot down the *G.I. Sheets*.

Of course, former members of the Belgian underground were in attendance. Dr. Maurice Verstraeten, Sylvie Derenne, Rene' Bouvigne, and of course, Arthur Derenne, were there. Also in attendance was Maurice Lamendin, who had hidden Jim and Don in his barn immediately after the crash. They were all able to tell their stories, and secrets from long ago were able to be revealed. They were able to walk the field where they had crashed, see the buildings and places where they had hidden, and were able to embrace each other. Don and Jim were able to tell their rescuers about the trip to Lille, and how they were captured by the Germans due to being betrayed by the French doctor.

It was a time to heal the old wounds from the war.

EPILOGUE

I'm always amazed about how seemingly random events in one's life seem to fall into place in order to make things happen, usually stuff that you hadn't planned to happen in the first place.

I've always been an airplane nut. I love flying them, reading about them, and talking about them. I have a particular passion for aviation history, and many years ago I was approached by my dear friend Dr. Gene Brunkhorst of Southeast Missouri State University about participating in a summer graduate workshop program that was targeting teachers, and showing them how to use aviation in their classrooms. Gene asked if I would be willing to do lectures regarding basic aerodynamics and aviation history. I jumped at the chance. Little did I know that I would be lecturing in this workshop for the next 17 summers, and I enjoyed every minute of it.

During one of the workshops, one of the participants brought in some newspaper clippings and photos documenting her father's story about going to Belgium to reunite with a community of people who had hidden him from the Germans. His B-17 had crashed near their village in 1944. Besides presenting me with an interesting story, this chance encounter would ultimately result in me being extremely blessed with meeting Donna. We ended up getting married several years later, and I became the son-in-law of Don and Jean Dinwiddie.

Don's story, to paraphrase something he liked to say, was just one of many. Each soldier, sailor, and airman had a story to tell about the war. All were very similar, but all were strikingly different in many ways.

One way of explaining this is the fact that all military men go through the same training that everyone in their particular branch experiences. They're all cookie-cutter similar after training. But then when thrust into the war, as hard as the military tried to suppress it, their personalities would shine through the olive drab. The more that I learned about the Fowler crew, the more evident this became, and I hope that the reader can see the various personalities of the individual crew members.

An added dimension to this came when I was able to go to Belgium and visit the area and some of the people who were involved in helping the men of the *G.I. Sheets*. It was 1988, and I went to Holland to visit my good friend and author Steven Ruffin, who was stationed near Amsterdam with the U.S. Air Force.

We drove south to Solre Saint Gery, Belgium to see the crash site. Don had called a couple of people to let them know that we were going to spend a day there.

When Steve and I arrived in the area, we stopped in Beaumont to have lunch before traveling the short distance to Solre Saint Gery. We randomly chose to stop at a small restaurant called Le Mouton Blanc because it looked pleasant, if for no other reason. When we sat down, it seemed as if there was a great deal of interest being shown in us by the other patrons and the staff. The waitress even seemed a little flustered when she was taking our orders.

The small town of Beaumont had a population of several thousand, so it was with great surprise that the waitress nervously asked us if we were "the Americans coming to visit Solre Saint Gery". It seemed that our reputation, such as it was, had proceeded us. It was our introduction to Belgian hospitality, and the high regard that the Belgian people have for Americans and what they still remembered about our role in the liberation of their country during World War Two.

After lunch, a phone call to our guide and interpreter, Anne Derignaux, set things in motion for the rest of the day. Anne came to retrieve us from the restaurant, and we drove to Solre Saint Gery and the monument that had been dedicated the year before. She took us to the studio of artist Denise Siquiet, who was instrumental in designing the monument. The four of us then went to the home of Sylvie Derenne. It was truly an honor to sit and talk to her and hear her stories of the war. I only regret that I

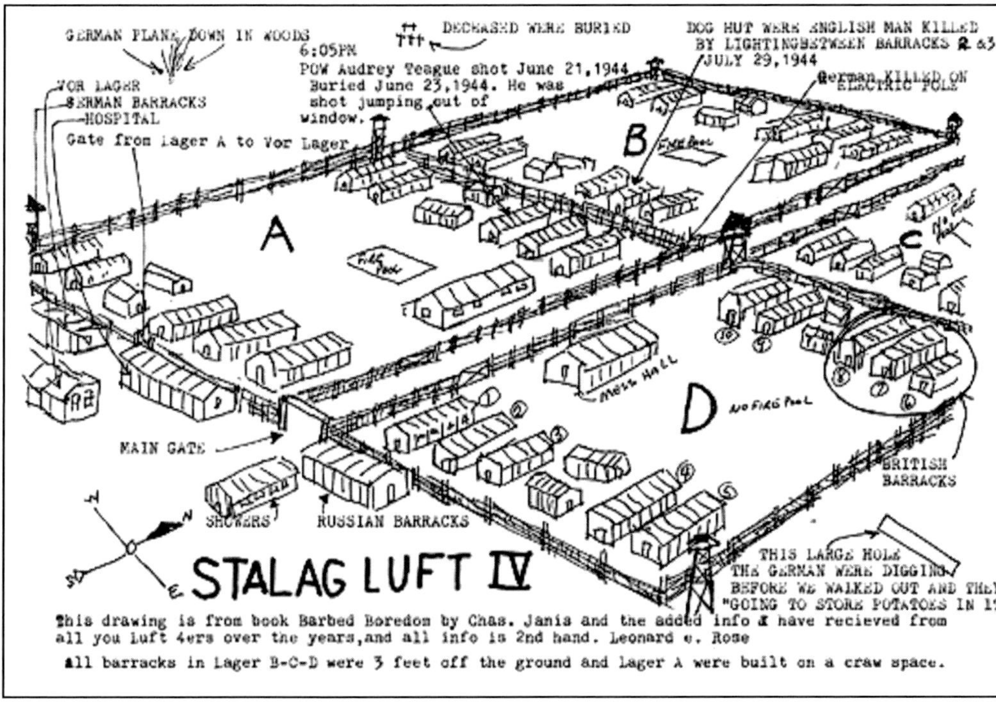

Drawing of the approximate layout of Stalag Luft IV.

New POWs arriving at Dulag Luft in Oberursel.

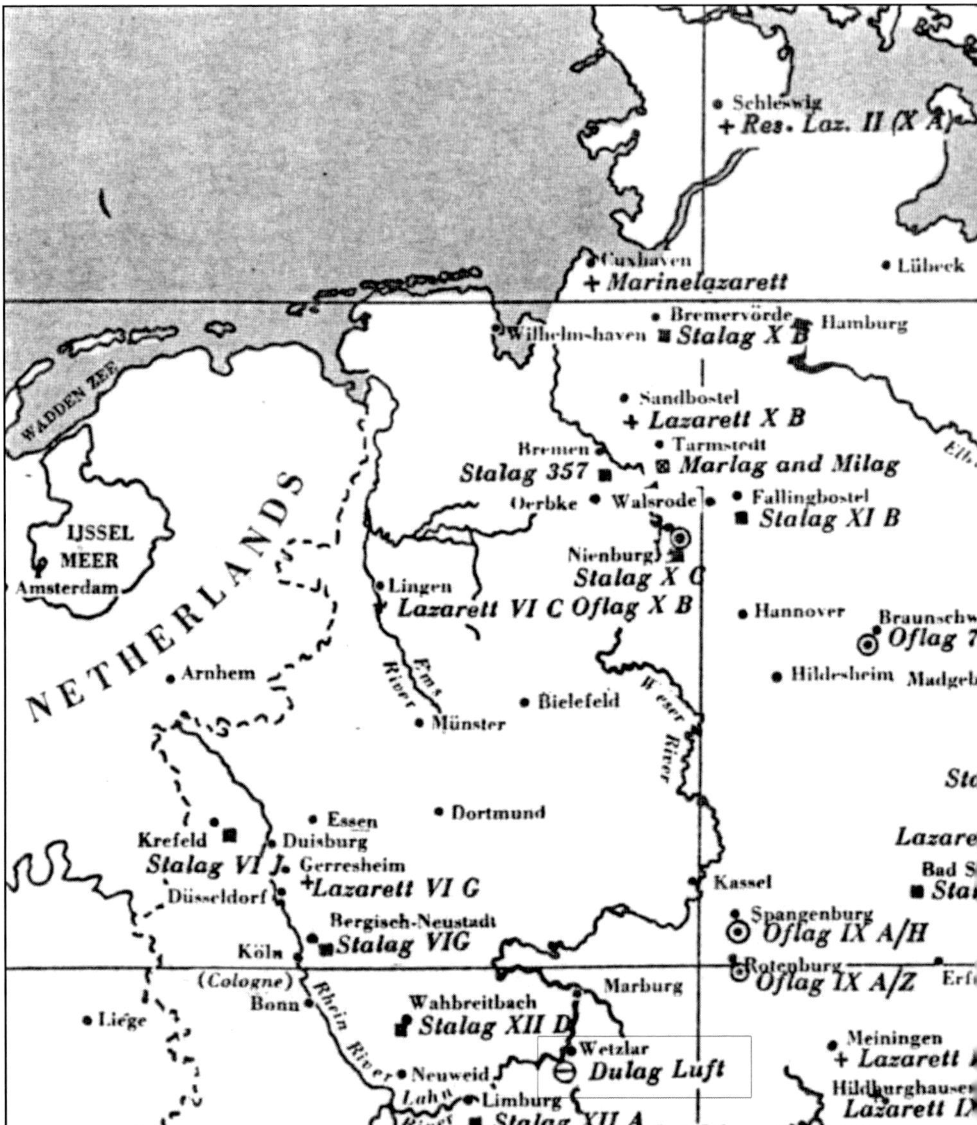

Locations of the German POW camps. Dulag Luft was where new prisoners were sent for classification and transfer. Stalag Luft IV is where Don was sent, and Stalag Luft I is where Jim Fowler was sent.

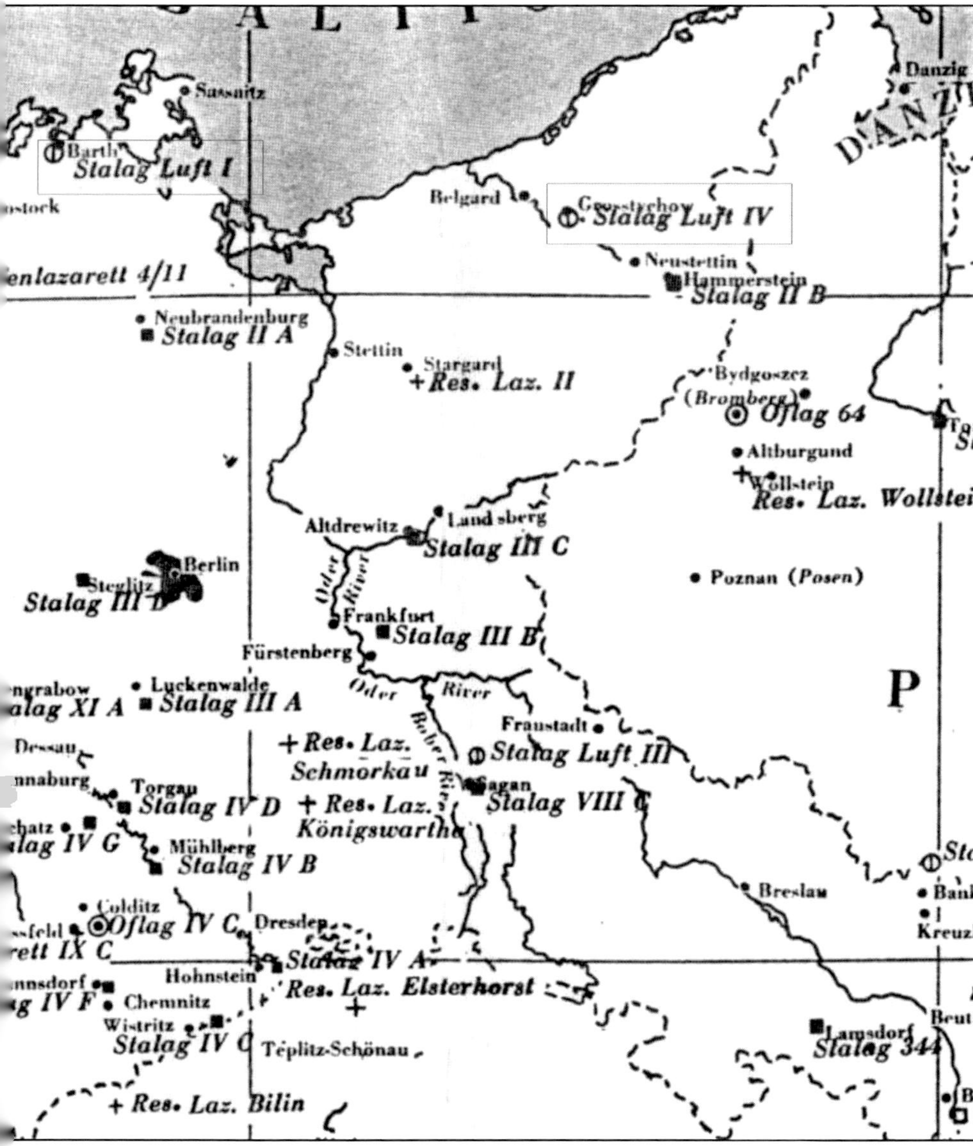
Sassnitz
Barth
Stalag Luft I
Danzig
Belgard
Stalag Luft IV
Neustettin
Hammerstein
Stalag II B
Neubrandenburg
Stalag II A
Stettin
Stargard
Res. Laz. II
Bydgoszcz
(Bromberg)
Oflag 64
Altburgund
Res. Laz. Wollstein
Altdrewitz
Landsberg
Stalag III C
Berlin
Poznan (Posen)
Frankfurt
Stalag III B
Fürstenberg
Luckenwalde
Stalag III A
Oder River
Fraustadt
Res. Laz. Schmorkau
Stalag Luft III
Torgau
Stalag IV D
Res. Laz. Königswarthe
Sagan
Stalag VIII C
Mühlberg
Stalag IV B
Breslau
Colditz
Oflag IV C
Dresden
Stalag IV A
Hohnstein
Res. Laz. Elsterhorst
Chemnitz
Wistritz
Stalag IV C
Teplitz-Schönau
Lamsdorf
Stalag 344
Res. Laz. Bilin
P

New prisoners at Dulag Luft. While the process was designed to intimidate new prisoners into giving up information, the Germans were not expecting the G.I.s and airmen to have any "secret" or important knowledge. While Geneva rules allowed the POWs to be there up to thirty days, most were there only three days at most before moving to a permanent Stalag.

Photo of Dulag Luft showing POWs herded into a "corral" similar (or maybe the same one) to that where Don reunited with former high school basketball opponent Robert "Buddy" Shaw from Fayette, Missouri.

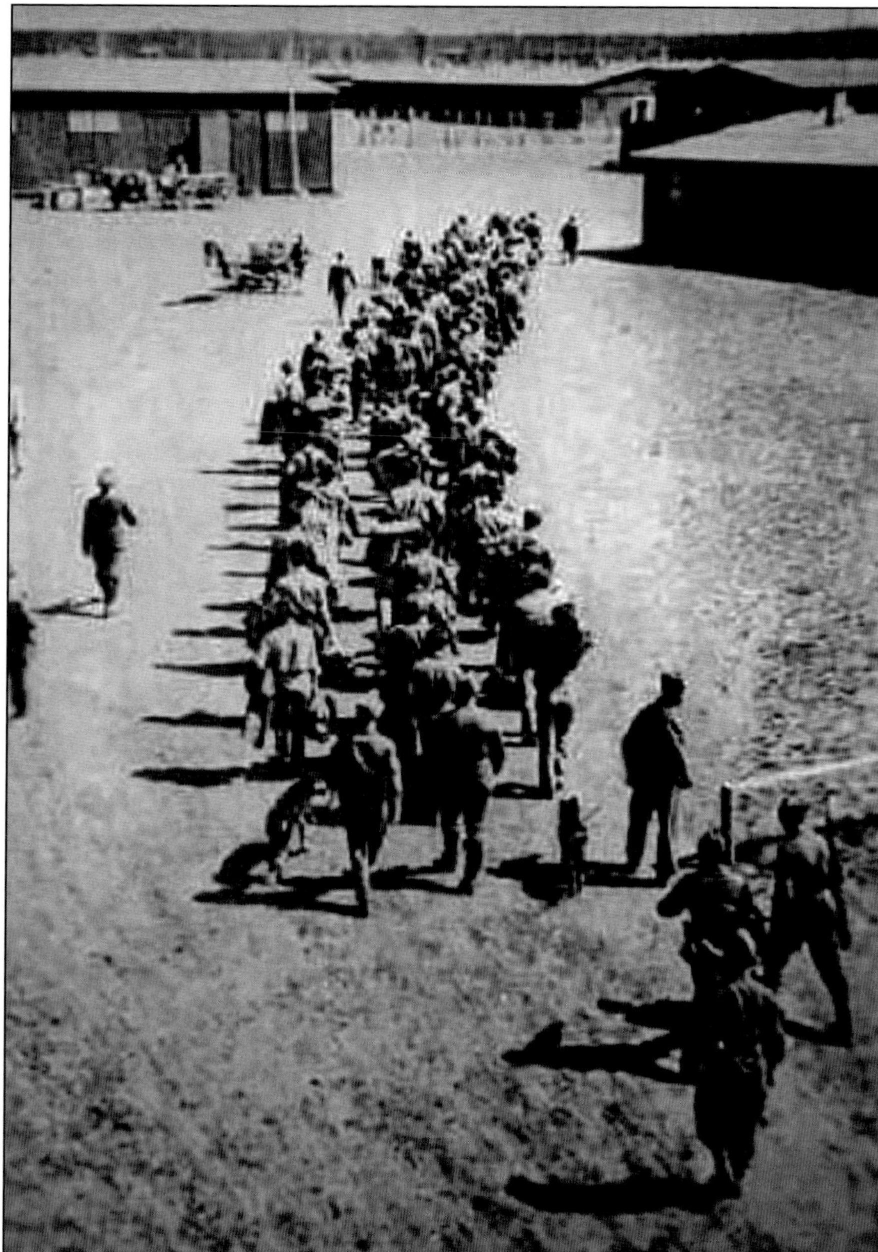

POWs being marched through the main entrance into Stalag Luft IV. When Don arrived at Luft IV, it was new with few prisoners. Within nine months, the population of POWs had grown to over 7,000. The sharp rise was mostly due to the land invasion after D-Day, June 6, 1944. While built to house aviators, it also became home to some ground troops.

Photo of Stalag Luft IV taken by Germans from a guard tower. This is "A" Lager, including from l-r: Barracks #5, #4, the latrine or washroom, then Barracks #3, #2, and #1.

Another "official" photo taken by the Germans showing POWs having fun in captivity. POWs did enjoy the diversion…boredom was always a problem.

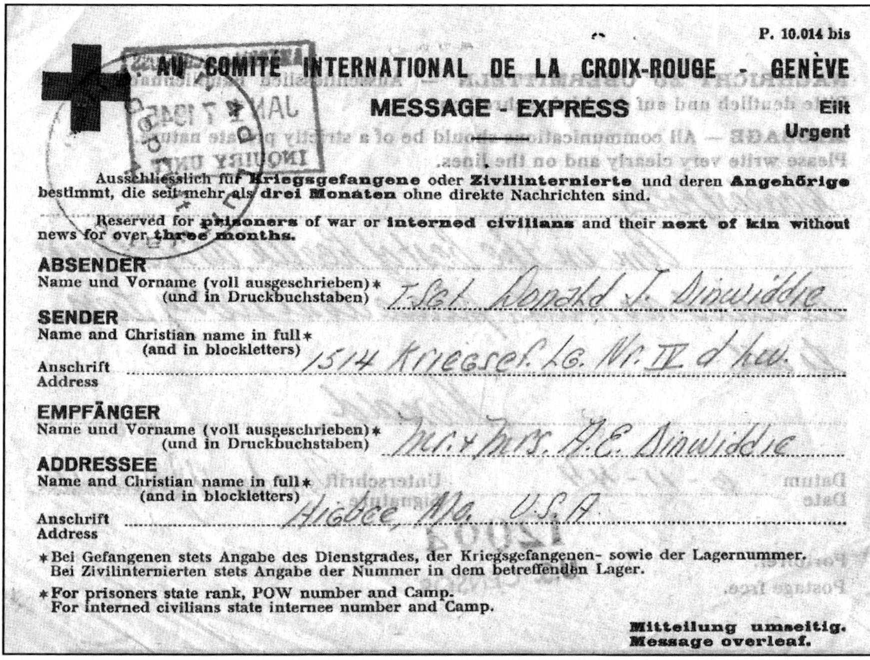

P. 10.014 bis

AU COMITÉ INTERNATIONAL DE LA CROIX-ROUGE - GENÈVE

MESSAGE - EXPRESS Eilt Urgent

JAN 17 1945 INQUIRY UNIT

Ausschliesslich für **Kriegsgefangene** oder **Zivilinternierte** und deren **Angehörige** bestimmt, die seit mehr als **drei Monaten** ohne direkte Nachrichten sind.

Reserved for **prisoners** of war or **interned civilians** and their **next of kin** without news for over **three months**.

ABSENDER
Name und Vorname (voll ausgeschrieben)* (und in Druckbuchstaben) T-Sgt. Donald J. Dinwiddie
SENDER
Name and Christian name in full* (and in blockletters)
Anschrift / Address 1514 Kriegsgef. Lg. Nr. IV d Luft.

EMPFÄNGER
Name und Vorname (voll ausgeschrieben)* (und in Druckbuchstaben) Mr. & Mrs. A.E. Dinwiddie
ADDRESSEE
Name and Christian name in full* (and in blockletters)
Anschrift / Address Higbee, Mo. U.S.A.

*Bei Gefangenen stets Angabe des Dienstgrades, der Kriegsgefangenen- sowie der Lagernummer. Bei Zivilinternierten stets Angabe der Nummer in dem betreffenden Lager.

*For prisoners state rank, POW number and Camp. For interned civilians state internee number and Camp.

Mitteilung umseitig. Message overleaf.

Front of "Kriegie Card" (prisoner mail) sent by Don to his parents.

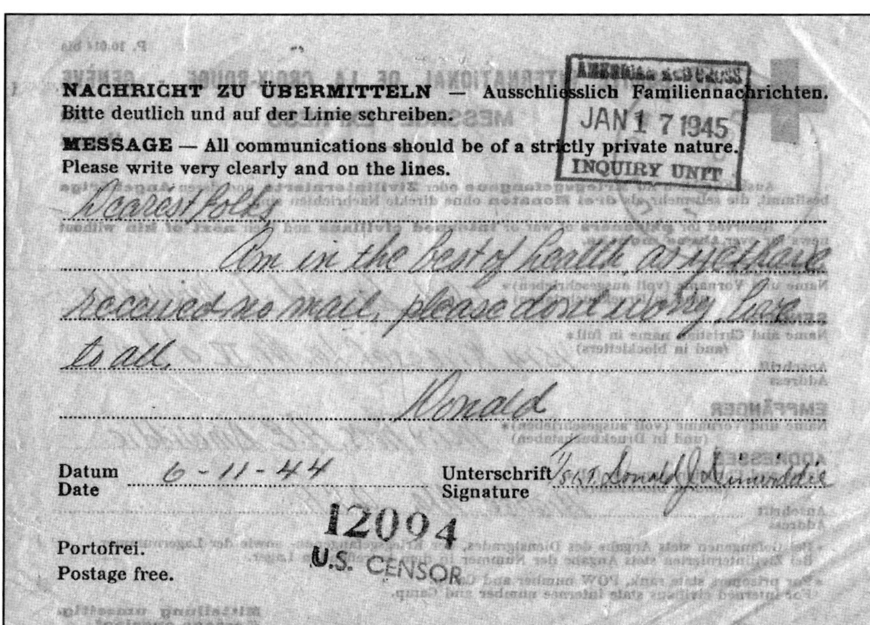

NACHRICHT ZU ÜBERMITTELN — Ausschliesslich Familiennachrichten.
Bitte deutlich und auf der Linie schreiben.

MESSAGE — All communications should be of a strictly private nature.
Please write very clearly and on the lines.

AMERICAN RED CROSS JAN 17 1945 INQUIRY UNIT

Dearest Folks
Am in the best of health as yet have received no mail, please don't worry. Love to all.
Donald

Datum / Date 6-11-44 Unterschrift / Signature T-Sgt. Donald J. Dinwiddie

Portofrei. Postage free.

12094 U.S. CENSOR

Note from Don saying he was in good health but had received no mail.

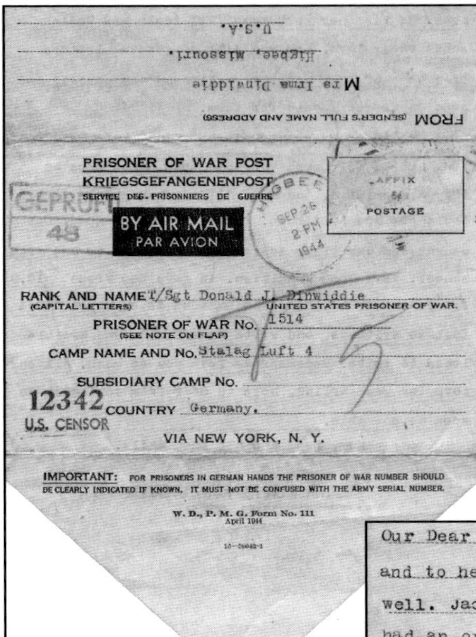
FROM (SENDER'S FULL NAME AND ADDRESS)
Mrs Irma Dinwiddie
Higbee, Missouri.
U.S.A.

PRISONER OF WAR POST
KRIEGSGEFANGENENPOST
SERVICE DES PRISONNIERS DE GUERRE
BY AIR MAIL
PAR AVION
AFFIX 5¢ POSTAGE

RANK AND NAME T/Sgt Donald J. Dinwiddie
(CAPITAL LETTERS) UNITED STATES PRISONER OF WAR.
PRISONER OF WAR No. 1514
(SEE NOTE ON FLAP)
CAMP NAME AND No. Stalag Luft 4
SUBSIDIARY CAMP No.
12342 COUNTRY Germany.
U.S. CENSOR
VIA NEW YORK, N. Y.

IMPORTANT: FOR PRISONERS IN GERMAN HANDS THE PRISONER OF WAR NUMBER SHOULD BE CLEARLY INDICATED IF KNOWN. IT MUST NOT BE CONFUSED WITH THE ARMY SERIAL NUMBER.
W. D., P. M. G. Form No. 111
April 1944

Official mail form for letter from Don's parents to Stalag Luft IV.

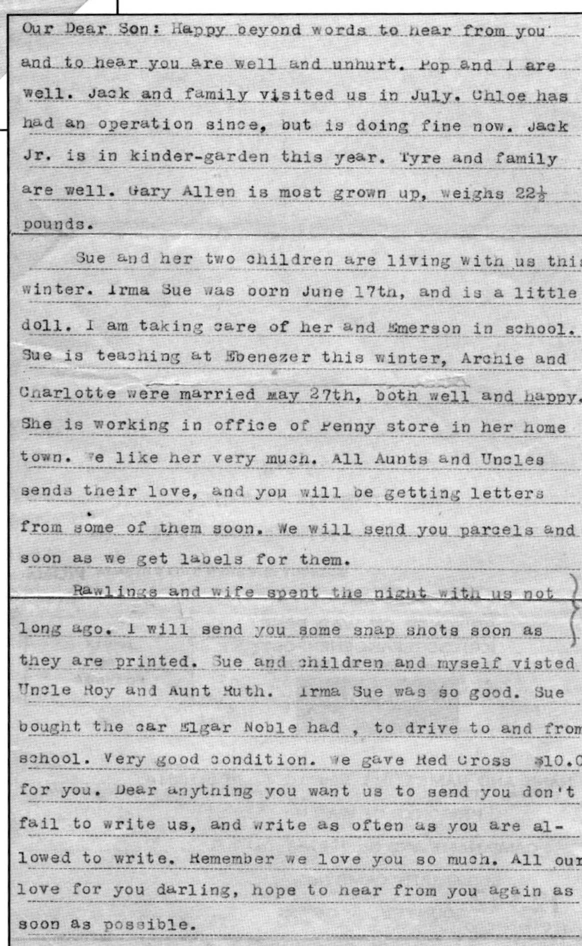
Our Dear Son: Happy beyond words to hear from you and to hear you are well and unhurt. Pop and I are well. Jack and family visited us in July. Chloe has had an operation since, but is doing fine now. Jack Jr. is in kinder-garden this year. Tyre and family are well. Gary Allen is most grown up, weighs 22½ pounds.

Sue and her two children are living with us this winter. Irma Sue was born June 17th, and is a little doll. I am taking care of her and Emerson in school. Sue is teaching at Ebenezer this winter, Archie and Charlotte were married May 27th, both well and happy. She is working in office of Penny store in her home town. We like her very much. All Aunts and Uncles sends their love, and you will be getting letters from some of them soon. We will send you parcels and soon as we get labels for them.

Rawlings and wife spent the night with us not long ago. I will send you some snap shots soon as they are printed. Sue and children and myself visted Uncle Roy and Aunt Ruth. Irma Sue was so good. Sue bought the car Elgar Noble had , to drive to and from school. Very good condition. We gave Red Cross $10.00 for you. Dear anything you want us to send you don't fail to write us, and write as often as you are al-lowed to write. Remember we love you so much. All our love for you darling, hope to hear from you again as soon as possible.

Mom, Pop, and all the family.

Letter from home to Don mailed September 29, 1944. Note that Barney Rawlings and his wife spent the night with Don's parents. Rawlings made it a point to talk to the families of all the other crew members after his return to the United States.

Typical POW bunk room at Stalag Luft IV.

Roll call at Stalag Luft IV. The term "lager" refers to a particular group of barracks buildings.

Beginning the "Long March", February 1945.

Going through a German town on the "Long March".

Typical of country roads used on the forced march.

Map of the Long March from Stalag Luft IV. The POWs and their guards marched eighty-six days and covered approximately 600 miles. The destination was Fallingbostel, near Hanover. That was reached, then the POWs were marched northeast, away from the approaching British and U.S. forces. Don's group was liberated at Gudow, near Hamburg.

Liberated POWs with British 8th Army Royal Dragoons at Gudow, Germany.

Jubilant American and British POWs liberated by British forces near Gudow, Germany.

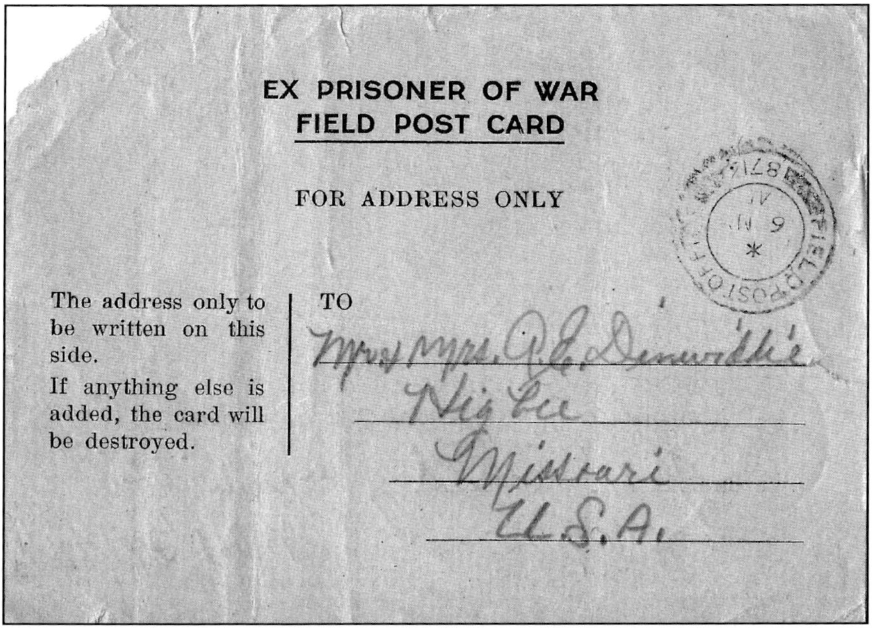

EX PRISONER OF WAR
FIELD POST CARD

FOR ADDRESS ONLY

The address only to be written on this side.
If anything else is added, the card will be destroyed.

TO
Mr & Mrs. R. C. Dinwiddie
Higbee
Missouri
U.S.A.

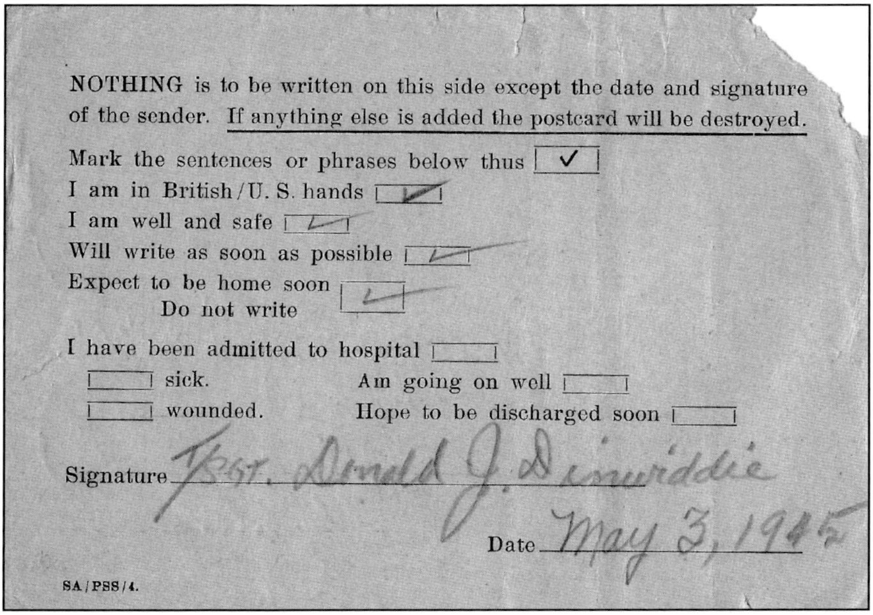

NOTHING is to be written on this side except the date and signature of the sender. If anything else is added the postcard will be destroyed.

Mark the sentences or phrases below thus ✓
I am in British/U. S. hands ✓
I am well and safe ✓
Will write as soon as possible ✓
Expect to be home soon
Do not write ✓

I have been admitted to hospital
sick. Am going on well
wounded. Hope to be discharged soon

Signature T/Sgt. Donald J. Dinwiddie

Date May 3, 1945

SA/PSS/4.

Ex-POW Field post card sent home by Don after being liberated by British forces at Gudow, Germany. He was liberated on May 2nd and the, card was sent May 3rd.

Camp Phillip Morris, one of the "cigarette camps" near Le Havre, France.

Camp Lucky Strike, one of the largest "cigarette camps", housed over 60,000 troops waiting to be shipped home. Don went to one of the cigarette camps before coming home, but which one is not known.

Don Dinwiddie after discharge from the Army Air Force. Note the aircrew wings or aerial gunner's wings on his left side (he was qualified to wear both; there were no radioman's wings at that time). On his right side is the Honorable Discharge from World War II badge.

Don and his mother Irma after his discharge and return home. Note the shoulder patch of the Army Air Force and the stripes showing the rank of Technical Sergeant.

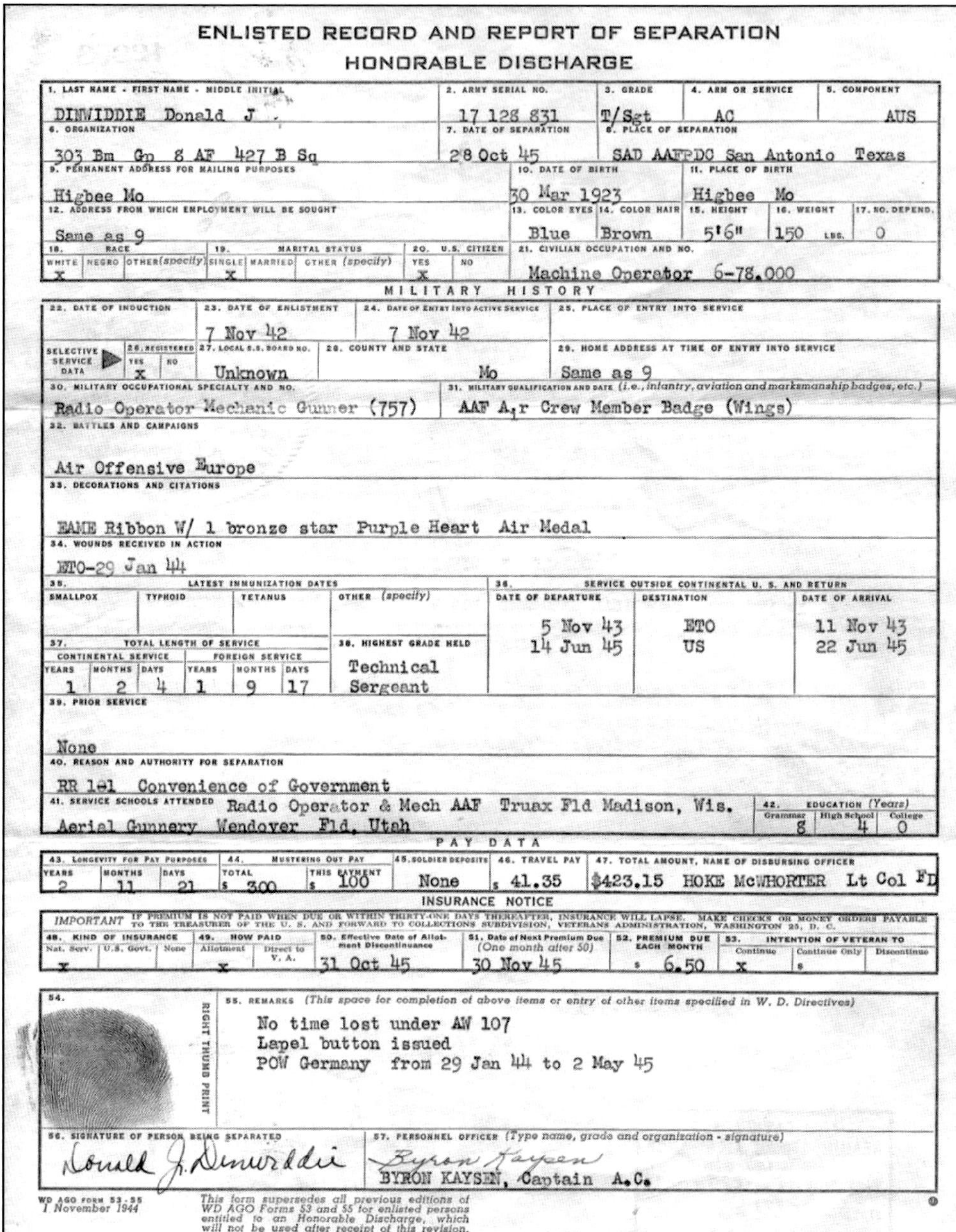

ENLISTED RECORD AND REPORT OF SEPARATION
HONORABLE DISCHARGE

1. LAST NAME - FIRST NAME - MIDDLE INITIAL: DINWIDDIE Donald J.
2. ARMY SERIAL NO.: 17 128 831
3. GRADE: T/Sgt
4. ARM OR SERVICE: AC
5. COMPONENT: AUS
6. ORGANIZATION: 303 Bm Gp 8 AF 427 B Sq
7. DATE OF SEPARATION: 28 Oct 45
8. PLACE OF SEPARATION: SAD AAFPDC San Antonio Texas
9. PERMANENT ADDRESS FOR MAILING PURPOSES: Higbee Mo
10. DATE OF BIRTH: 30 Mar 1923
11. PLACE OF BIRTH: Higbee Mo
12. ADDRESS FROM WHICH EMPLOYMENT WILL BE SOUGHT: Same as 9
13. COLOR EYES: Blue
14. COLOR HAIR: Brown
15. HEIGHT: 5'6"
16. WEIGHT: 150 LBS.
17. NO. DEPEND.: 0
18. RACE: WHITE x | NEGRO | OTHER (specify)
19. MARITAL STATUS: SINGLE x | MARRIED | OTHER (specify)
20. U.S. CITIZEN: YES x | NO
21. CIVILIAN OCCUPATION AND NO.: Machine Operator 6-78.000

MILITARY HISTORY

22. DATE OF INDUCTION:
23. DATE OF ENLISTMENT: 7 Nov 42
24. DATE OF ENTRY INTO ACTIVE SERVICE: 7 Nov 42
25. PLACE OF ENTRY INTO SERVICE:
SELECTIVE SERVICE DATA — 26. REGISTERED: YES x | NO
27. LOCAL S.S. BOARD NO.: Unknown
28. COUNTY AND STATE: Mo
29. HOME ADDRESS AT TIME OF ENTRY INTO SERVICE: Same as 9
30. MILITARY OCCUPATIONAL SPECIALTY AND NO.: Radio Operator Mechanic Gunner (757)
31. MILITARY QUALIFICATION AND DATE (i.e., infantry, aviation and marksmanship badges, etc.): AAF Air Crew Member Badge (Wings)
32. BATTLES AND CAMPAIGNS: Air Offensive Europe
33. DECORATIONS AND CITATIONS: EAME Ribbon W/ 1 bronze star Purple Heart Air Medal
34. WOUNDS RECEIVED IN ACTION: ETO-29 Jan 44
35. LATEST IMMUNIZATION DATES: SMALLPOX | TYPHOID | TETANUS | OTHER (specify)

36. SERVICE OUTSIDE CONTINENTAL U. S. AND RETURN

DATE OF DEPARTURE	DESTINATION	DATE OF ARRIVAL
5 Nov 43	ETO	11 Nov 43
14 Jun 45	US	22 Jun 45

37. TOTAL LENGTH OF SERVICE

CONTINENTAL SERVICE			FOREIGN SERVICE		
YEARS	MONTHS	DAYS	YEARS	MONTHS	DAYS
1	2	4	1	9	17

38. HIGHEST GRADE HELD: Technical Sergeant
39. PRIOR SERVICE: None
40. REASON AND AUTHORITY FOR SEPARATION: RR 1-1 Convenience of Government
41. SERVICE SCHOOLS ATTENDED: Radio Operator & Mech AAF Truax Fld Madison, Wis. Aerial Gunnery Wendover Fld, Utah
42. EDUCATION (Years): Grammar 8 | High School 4 | College 0

PAY DATA

43. LONGEVITY FOR PAY PURPOSES: YEARS 2 | MONTHS 11 | DAYS 21
44. MUSTERING OUT PAY: TOTAL $ 300 | THIS PAYMENT $ 100
45. SOLDIER DEPOSITS: None
46. TRAVEL PAY: $ 41.35
47. TOTAL AMOUNT, NAME OF DISBURSING OFFICER: $423.15 HOKE McWHORTER Lt Col FD

INSURANCE NOTICE

IMPORTANT: IF PREMIUM IS NOT PAID WHEN DUE OR WITHIN THIRTY-ONE DAYS THEREAFTER, INSURANCE WILL LAPSE. MAKE CHECKS OR MONEY ORDERS PAYABLE TO THE TREASURER OF THE U. S. AND FORWARD TO COLLECTIONS SUBDIVISION, VETERANS ADMINISTRATION, WASHINGTON 25, D. C.

48. KIND OF INSURANCE: Nat. Serv. x | U.S. Govt. | None
49. HOW PAID: Allotment x | Direct to V. A.
50. Effective Date of Allotment Discontinuance: 31 Oct 45
51. Date of Next Premium Due (One month after 50): 30 Nov 45
52. PREMIUM DUE EACH MONTH: $ 6.50
53. INTENTION OF VETERAN TO: Continue x | Continue Only $ | Discontinue

54. RIGHT THUMB PRINT

55. REMARKS (This space for completion of above items or entry of other items specified in W. D. Directives)
No time lost under AW 107
Lapel button issued
POW Germany from 29 Jan 44 to 2 May 45

56. SIGNATURE OF PERSON BEING SEPARATED: Donald J. Dinwiddie
57. PERSONNEL OFFICER (Type name, grade and organization - signature): Byron Kaysen
BYRON KAYSEN, Captain A.C.

WD AGO FORM 53-55
1 November 1944

This form supersedes all previous editions of WD AGO Forms 53 and 55 for enlisted persons entitled to an Honorable Discharge, which will not be used after receipt of this revision.

Don's official discharge from the Army Air Force. Note the back pay that was given to him upon discharge. The $423 in 1945 would be equal to over $6,000 in 2020.

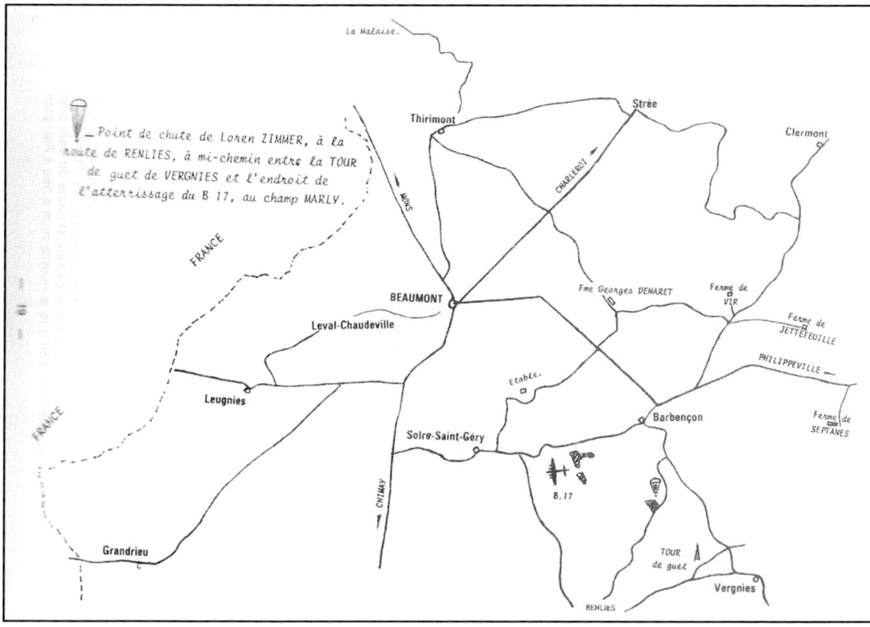

Hand-drawn map of the crash site area found in the booklet distributed at the monument dedication. Note that the B-17 drawing marks the crash site on Marly's Field, and the small parachute marks where Loren Zimmer landed in farmer Albert Rolin's bog. Note the location of the German observation tower southeast of crash site near Vergenies.

Monument to the Fowler crew built by the citizens of Solre Saint Gery and dedicated in June 1987, with several members of the crew present.

Don (right) and Jim Fowler being interviewed for Belgian television at the monument dedication in June 1987.

At the monument dedication in Belgium, June 1987. Front row, l-r: Jim Fowler, Jean Dinwiddie, Don Dinwiddie, Barney Rawlings, Elaine Rawlings, and Curtis Finley, Jr. Back row, l-r: Mrs. Curtis Finley, Jr, Margaret Fowler, and Lucille Finley, widow of Curtis Finley, Sr.

Madame Jean Dogne, who was one of the underground members who hid Don and Jim in 1944. Photo June 1987.

Don and Jean Dinwiddie in Belgium, June 1987.

Loren and Betty Zimmer with monument, Belgium 1988.

The only known wartime photo of French traitor and Nazi collaborator, Marcel Deneque. Deneque was tried, convicted, and sentenced to death for being responsible for the capture of over 300 Belgian and French underground members and Allied airmen (including Don and Jim). His actions resulted in the capture of Dr. Leon Baron and his wife, creating the illusion that the doctor and his wife were working for the Nazis. He was also thought to be the man responsible for the capture of Sylvie Derenne and her husband and others in the southwestern Belgium area. He was murdered in a French prison before his death sentence was carried out. Photo courtesy of Greg Celerse.

A young Winston Churchill (foreground, far right) being held as a POW in South Africa in the Boer War, 1899. He escaped from captivity and managed to travel nearly 300 miles before reaching British troops. He was helped along the way by people friendly to the British cause, and his memory of this aid caused him to create a division in British Intelligence to promote the use of friendly partisans if and when war with Germany became a reality.

Painted in all black, a B-24 takes off from RAF Harrington. The B-24 was the workhorse of the Carpetbagger missions. Note the absence of nose, belly, and waist guns. The agents, nicknamed "Joes", were dropped out the bottom in the hole made by the removal of the belly turret (normally located on the bottom of the fuselage below the star). Because of the nickname "Joe", the hole in the aircraft naturally became known as the "Joe Hole".

Douglas A-26 similar to those used by the Carpetbaggers primarily for insertion of agents deep into German-occupied territory. These missions were primarily flown after D-Day, and most were into Germany. The speed and maneuverability of the A-26 was definitely a plus in getting into enemy territory quickly and then making a run for home. Agents were not happy with having to be dropped from the bomb bay like a bomb, but because of the design of the aircraft, this was the most expedient method.

A British DeHavilland Mosquito in United States markings that was being used by the Carpetbagger group at RAF Harrington. As described earlier in this book, the Mosquito was extremely fast at high altitude, and could outrun most of the piston-engine fighters that the Germans were using. It was made of wood, was lightweight, and was powered by the Rolls-Royce Merlin engine, the same engine that powered the P-51D Mustang. As typical of the night-flying Carpetbagger aircraft, this one is painted black to avoid detection by German gunners and night fighters. American pilots typically didn't like the Mosquito when first flying it in training because it was very tricky to handle on takeoff. The powerful engines tended to cause a rapid swing of the nose if power was applied too quickly and if the pilot was too slow in reacting. After becoming accustomed to the Mossie, the Yank pilots came to love flying it as much as the Brits.

This Carpetbagger Mosquito was used as a high-altitude platform for sending and receiving clandestine radio messages to agents behind enemy lines during "Operation Red Stocking". The two men in the photograph are the pilot and navigator. An additional crew member was the radio operator. The crew was normally American.

British Westland Lysander used for clandestine missions, usually to retrieve agents within enemy territory. It was very capable in short-field operations and could carry three passengers as well as the pilot.

Left-side view of a Lysander showing the ladder built onto the fuselage to provide quick entry for airmen being retrieved from enemy territory.

Bomb-shaped containers for dropping supplies to the members of the underground. The containers were dropped out of the bomb bays with parachutes attached. The containers were so well built that they could protect high-explosives and ammunition safely.

Ground personnel loading drop containers in the bomb bay of a Carpetbagger B-24.

This photo is rare for two reasons: 1) It is a daylight drop, which was unusual, and probably was made some weeks after D-Day when the Germans were in retreat; and, 2) the aircraft dropping the containers was a B-17, not the usual drop aircraft. It was known that B-17 was used, but rarely. It could not carry the same load as the B-24 could, but the B-17 could fly more slowly and was easier to control at slower speeds than the B-24.

British Mosquito from the "Three Witches" unit. Like the Mosquitoes flown by the Carpetbaggers, these aircraft were used for clandestine radio missions. Note the silhouettes of witches on broomsticks painted below the cockpit window. One witch equals one mission. It is also interesting to see two swastikas painted on the fuselage, usually denoting two German aircraft destroyed. The Mosquito was an all-purpose aircraft capable of carrying bombs or used as an attack fighter. With the proper radar equipment, it was also used as a night fighter and could be a formidable opponent against German aircraft day or night.

Uniform patch worn by pilots and crew members of the very secret IS9 WEA unit, informally known as "The Three Witches".

This photo shows three members of the Royal Canadian Army. The man in the center is General Harold Crerar, Commander in Chief of Canadian Forces in World War II. The officer to the right is Captain George Swan, Royal Canadian Air Force. Swan was assigned to fly some of the clandestine radio flights over Europe after the D-Day invasion, hence the wearing of the "Three Witches" patch on his shoulder. The patch was only in existence from October 1944 to June 26, 1945. It was designed by a Dutch Lieutenant who was attached to IS9 WEA after the liberation of South Netherlands. This is the only known photo showing it being worn by a military officer. The patch is one of the rarest pieces of military memorabilia from World War II.

According to OSS files, this is a Jedburgh team retrieving supplies dropped by a Carpetbagger mission behind the lines in France.

A Jedburgh team, probably in France or Belgium. Note the lightweight sub-machine guns that were the usual weapon of choice.

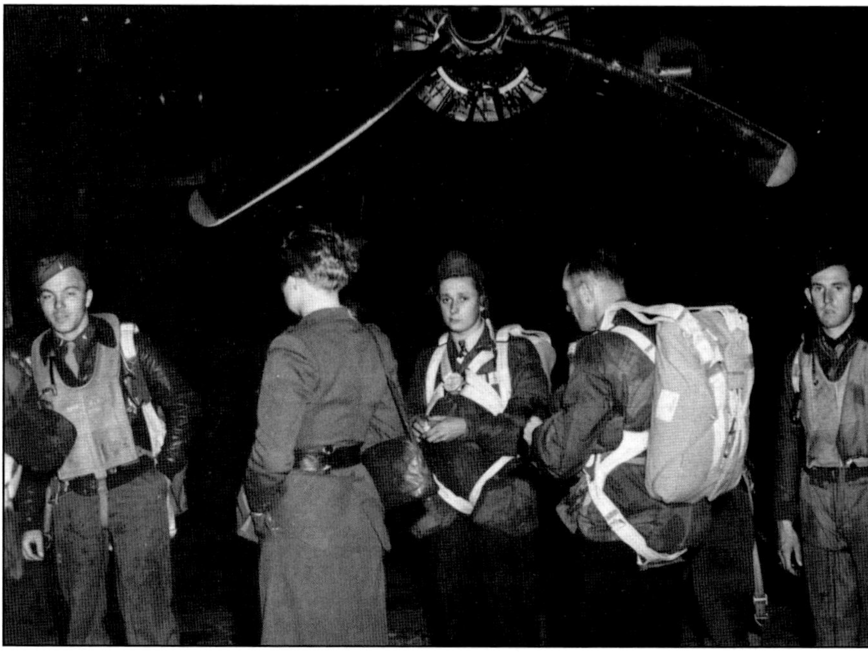

Two agents (wearing parachutes) preparing for departure on a Carpetbagger B-24. The two men (far left and far right) wearing the flight gear are part of the crew, and the woman in the foreground with back to camera was probably the driver who took the agents to the takeoff point. Agents were normally delivered to the airfield and the aircraft in a vehicle with blacked-out windows so they would not know their departure point, and thus could not reveal this secret information if captured.

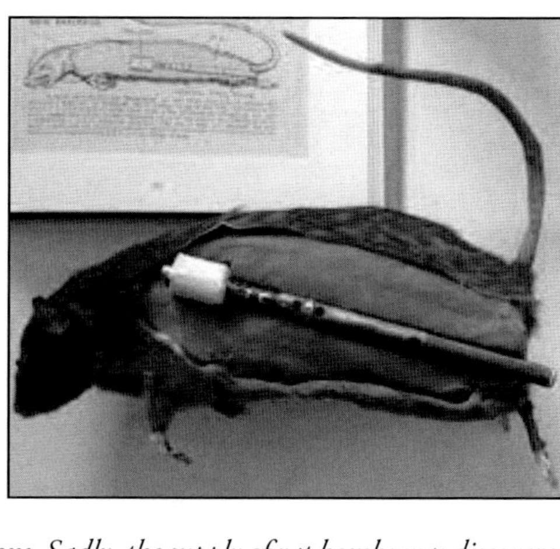

The exploding rat, a sabotage device designed by British Intelligence to be used against the Germans. The idea was for the explosive-filled rat carcass to be thrown in coal storage in German headquarters buildings by partisans. As the coal was being thrown into furnaces, the rat would be found and disposed of in the fire. The fuse in the rat was temperature sensitive and would set off the plastic explosive filling the rat's body when tossed in the fire. The idea was typical of the "out of the box" thinking of members of the intelligence organizations. Sadly, the supply of rat bombs was discovered by the Germans before they could be distributed and put to use.

Moe Berg, the Boston Red Sox catcher who was a spy. Berg took photos and movies in Tokyo while on a baseball trip to Japan in 1940, prior to the war. The photos proved valuable during the war for planning bombing attacks. Later, he was employed by the OSS and ferreted out information from German civilian scientists who were working on Hitler's secret projects, including his attempt to build the atomic bomb.

Christopher Clayton Hutton, the model for "Q" of 007 fame. Hutton worked with British Intelligence to develop all sorts of "spy gadgets" that could be used by evading airmen or agents dropped behind enemy lines. Among the items in this photo, the most prominent are the aviator's boots. The high tops included a hidden knife, and the tops could be cut along a scored line that allowed them to be removed to make the boots into a pair of regular slippers that would not be as noticeable during evasion. Other items that Hutton developed were fountain pens and pencils that concealed hidden stiletto blades, small compasses hidden in uniform buttons, and maps hidden in decks of playing cards. These are but a few of the inventions of Hutton and his team.

A British uniform button that conceals a magnetic compass. The button unscrews by turning it to the right instead of the customary left hand direction, thus hiding it from the prying eyes of a German prison guard or policeman who might try to unscrew it the customary way.

The name is Fleming...Ian Fleming. The creator of James Bond was a real secret agent, working for British Intelligence in World War II. An officer in the Royal Navy, he was involved in several clandestine operations, thus giving him the basis for the legendary 007. No chapter on British Intelligence is complete without his photo.

know more now about the situation than I knew in 1988. Gosh, what questions I could ask her now! The visit to Solre Saint Gery was a stop on the road trip that Steve and I took across Belgium and into the area of the Ardennes where the Battle of the Bulge was fought. If I were to take the same 1988 journey with today's knowledge, I could have spent weeks in Solre Saint Gery alone. But the afternoon visit with Sylvie and Denise and Anne was enough to light the fire that would burn in me about the last mission of the *G.I. Sheets*, and what Don and his friends had gone through.

With the advent of the internet it, was easier to seek and find information, even though one had to exercise care in deciding the accuracy and veracity of it. One of the best sites that I came across years later was the excellent website of the 303rd Bomb Group put together by Gary Moncur in 1997.

Gary's father Vernon was a pilot in the 303rd, so the website is a labor of love and respect, dedicated to the memories of those who served in that unit. It was a great source of information that started me in the right direction.

Another great source was Barney Rawlings. I was able to communicate with him before his death in 2004. Barney shared stories with me about the war and his early days of flying with TWA. I want to take this opportunity to thank him for the copy of his book, *Off We Went (Into the Wild Blue Yonder)* that he graciously gave me. I'll also state here that many of his stories, photos, and recollections were the springboard for more research, and I want to credit him for that. Several of the photos found here were his, and are so noted. I tried with no success to locate Barney's son Roger in order to get official permission to use the photos. Since I couldn't ask for his permission, then I'll beg for his forgiveness if he ever reads this.

Some other photos were from official Army Air Force archives, and others were taken from a pamphlet that the Belgian residents had put together for the celebration and dedication of the monument. A sincere thanks to them.

Since the events of that I've written about took place over seventy-five years ago and I obviously wasn't present, I had to use some creativity to fill in certain areas that were not crucial to the actual story. One such scenario was what happened on the morning of the mission, before takeoff. What I described prior to departure regarding the preparation of the aircraft, and the dialogue between pilots and crew was typical of what would've happened. The events that took place in the actual combat phase of the mission were more or less accurate, and told to me by Barney and Don.

The information concerning what happened after the crash at Marly's Field on the outskirts of Solre Saint Gery is drawn from the accounts of several people. The accounts of Barney and Don certainly played a part, but the crew members were soon isolated from each other, so after they were taken from the site, the crew could only know what happened to themselves, not the others. A case in point would be the situation of Barney and Curt Finley. They ran off to the woods to hide, and neither was seen again. Until Barney made it back to England, nobody knew where he was.

When he did make it back to England, he had no idea what the situation was with his crew except that they were all alive after the crash with the probable exception of Jackson. It was a confusing situation for everyone involved.

Only after many years and certain events did things become more clear. Visiting and speaking to Sylvie Derenne was a huge help. She mentioned to me about a man who was the friend of a girl that worked for her, and in looking back, she felt that he was probably a Nazi collaborator. This man, who was in and out of the area but did not live locally, was probably responsible for the arrest of her and her husband by the Gestapo in 1944. On several occasions she had hidden some of the downed airmen in the attic of her shop, and the girl knew about them. She also told me that she felt that the capture of Don and Jim were connected to this man. That's all I had to go on for several years. I later had the information that showed that the girl working for Sylvie was probably Anne-Marie Bouffault. I assumed that the man she was referring to was probably Amboise Baudart, who was mentioned earlier as a Belgian who tried to impress on Anne-Marie's family that he was working for the underground. I later found out that I was probably mistaken on this and shouldn't have made that assumption. Baudart was from another Belgian village several miles to the north of Solre Saint

Gery, and was surely known. Apparently there was another man, who was probably working with Baudart, and who was responsible for the infiltration of the escape lines in the Solre Saint Gery area.

After Don's passing in 2005, although I was eager to write down his war experiences, I had hit a roadblock. I wasn't finding any new information, and I had run out of sources. I was almost to the point of having to accept the realization that perhaps I'd never find anything more than I had already discovered.

One of the things that got me back on track was the actual final moments of the *G.I. Sheets* after it flew out of the cloud cover over the German fighter base at Florennes. The more I thought about this, the more it intrigued me. If nothing else, the Germans were great at keeping records, and I wondered if I could find any information about the unit stationed there. I knew from American records that there was only one bomber shot down over Belgium on January 29, 1944, and that had to be the *G.I. Sheets.*

Through the help of a couple of historians that I had connected with over the internet, I was able to find that Jg 26 was the unit based at Florennes at the time in question. I also found that German records also showed that there was only one B-17 shot down in that area on January 29. I was now certain that it had to be the *G.I. Sheets.*

I was able to track down the records of Jg 26 for that day, and found that a B-17G was shot down by two Luftwaffe pilots in that area on that day, Oberleutnant Wolfgang Neu and his wingman, Oberleutnant Kurt Kranefeld. I hoped that they were still alive and that I would be able to get in contact with them, but I found additional records to show that neither lived through the war.

Neu was not a neophyte pilot at the time of the encounter with the *G.I. Sheets.* He was credited with shooting down twelve Allied aircraft before he himself was shot down and killed by an American P-47 in April of 1944. His wingman, Kranefeld, was also killed two months after Neu.

The question had always lingered in my mind as to why they stopped shooting at the Fowler plane when they could have easily blown it out of the sky. Barney always said that he felt like they knew that the plane was doomed and didn't want to do anymore harm to the crew than necessary. He always thought that the victory roll performed over the crashed B-17 on Marly's Field was indicative of that. After learning of the "false aviator" that showed up in Barbencon at the same time of the crash, I wondered if there was another scenario.

The Germans were very concerned about when and where the inevitable Allied ground invasion would take place. They knew that Allied spies and operatives were infiltrating western Europe, and they wanted to slow down the process if they couldn't stop it completely. They knew that the infiltrators were coming in through various means (Operation Jedburgh, as mentioned earlier), and were being aided by the French, Dutch, and Belgian underground cells. The same people who were helping downed aviators escape were also bringing the spies into German-occupied territory. As I stated earlier, by early 1944, the Germans were probably more interested in the infiltration of Allied operatives than catching evading airmen. The Germans knew that there were masses of equipment and troops in England preparing for a land invasion, and these infiltrators were the spearhead.

Knowing that the Germans were trying to break into the underground and knowing about the presence of the "false airmen" (not only the one in Barbecon, but others, also), I tend to think that there were contingencies in place for the Germans to exploit the right situation.

If the right scenario presented itself, there were probably German agents ready to pose as downed airmen at a moment's notice. The situation with the *G.I. Sheets* was perfect. It was cut off from its formation, damaged almost to the point of being unflyable. It popped out of the clouds directly over a Luftwaffe base. Not only had all that happened, but most of it took place where it was clearly visible from a German observation tower.

To make the situation even more appropriate to the German plan, Zimmer had bailed out, and would've been seen doing so by the FW-190 pilots, and probably by observers in the observation tower near the crash site. Could there have been orders given to Neu and Kranefeld to try to force the bomber down, and do it with minimum damage to plane and crew? I certainly think that this could be a possibility. For the purposes of the Germans, it would be more advantageous for the bomber crew to successfully escape than for them to be captured. The almost casual visit by the lone German soldier from the observation tower shortly after the crash also lends credence to this plan. He showed up, checked the papers of Dr. Verstraeten, gave the plane a cursory inspection, then left. He wasn't interested in the crew that had apparently escaped, and only saw two injured men and one apparently dead one. Most of the Germans would have known that a B-17 was crewed by 10 men, not three. One would think that the area around Solre Saint Gery would've been crawling with Germans searching for the missing crewmen. Certainly, the members of the underground in the village thought this would be happening soon, hence the rapid removal of the Americans with minor wounds who could be moved. So was the immediate attempt to destroy the plane.

As I began researching, I didn't know much about the French or Belgian underground and knew nothing about the workings of the escape lines. This aspect of the war became more clear after finding a French-English translation of some entries in a book written by a Belgian author about the underground activities in that country. He had solicited stories from some of the people who had helped hide the men of the Fowler crew, and the information gleaned from their anecdotal statements help put together a picture of what happened.

Their information, coupled with the information related by Barney and Don, finally painted an excellent picture of what exactly happened for the next several months after the crash. Because there were different escape lines working in the area, with different "handlers" working with the men, they were not in close contact. They did, however, stay in communication by way of some individuals who were common to several lines. Sylvie Derenne was one such person. She would travel to various hideouts to cut the hair of the hidden airmen, and would deliver messages from the other men.

Dr. Verstraeten was another person who knew the big picture of what was going on. In spite of the few people in the underground that seemed to have a lot of knowledge about the hidden aviators, most of the underground members had very limited information. By the very nature of what they did, the compartmentalization protected their identity and what they did. Not many knew the entire story of what they did as a whole, but only the individual members knew the part that they themselves played.

They typically harbored a hidden airman for awhile, then the man would be moved to another location. The members of the escape line did not usually know where a man came from or where he was going next. On the night of April 13, 1944, things started coming apart for some of the underground.

The Gestapo sent agents to search the house of Dr. Verstraeten, and questioned his neighbor, Madam Bouvigne, on suspicion of hiding American airmen. Having found no evidence, they were then left alone. But Sylvie Derenne and her husband were arrested, along with her assistant, Anne-Marie Bouffault. Despite these devastating events, none of the men of the Fowler crew were discovered.

As mentioned earlier, some of the escape lines felt that the ground invasion was imminent, and the evadees were being held in place rather than moved along the path toward England. Within the next three weeks after the Gestapo shakedown of April 13th, Jim Fowler and Don, however, were getting prepared to be moved.

Don and Jim were moved from Belgium into France, and turned over to the French underground for the next journey on their way back to England. On May 13, 1945 they were being moved to Lille, France, the next "station".

As they were being driven through Lille by the doctor and his wife, who were residents of that French town, they hadn't traveled far before their car was stopped by a German roadblock. It was very clear that the Germans knew that the men traveling with the French couple were Americans. They took Jim and Don out of the car and sent the doctor and his wife on their way. As mentioned earlier, both men were certain that they had been betrayed by the French couple. Don was sure of this for the rest of his life. At this point, my research hit a dead end.

I posted a comment on the 303rd Bomb Group website sometime after Don's passing regarding his capture and betrayal by the French doctor. It was just a comment to share with others, and I was not expecting to have a bombshell dropped on me.

One Sunday afternoon after returning home from the airport and a flight in my plane, I was pulling into the garage when Donna came out suddenly with the phone in her hand. She excitedly said that I had a phone call from France. I thought she was kidding.

There was indeed a man on the phone calling from France. The man identified himself as Greg Celerse, a French author and historian who had seen my post on the 303rd BG site, and told me that he had come across some incredible information that he knew I would want to have.

Greg was from the town of Lille, and was researching the topic of how French Nazi sympathizers had been hunted down and prosecuted by the French government after the war. Nazi collaborators were considered the worst kind of criminal, and the government was ruthless in their hunt for them. He said that during his research, he came across one of the most dangerous collaborators of all, a man named Marcel Deneque. Deneque had actually been born in Germany, but moved to France in the late 1920s. When Hitler came into power, he quietly aligned himself with the Nazi movement. When the war started, he worked for the Nazis as an agent, infiltrating organizations and exposing members of the French underground. Greg had been particularly interested in Deneque because of his notorious reputation, and also because he was from Lille, Greg's hometown, as well as home to Dr. Baron and his wife.

Greg had discovered that soon after the war, Deneque left his wife and young daughter and hid from the French government's efforts to track him down. He had deserted his family in order to protect himself.

So heinous were his crimes that the French tried him in absentia and sentenced him to death. Many years later, the government basically stopped tracking French Nazi collaborators, and Deneque came out of hiding and slipped back into Lille to see his family. As luck would have it, a man on the street recognized him and reported his presence to the police. Soon one of the most well-known French traitors was arrested.

It was suspected that Deneque's work for the Nazis had resulted in over 300 underground members and Allied aviators being captured by the Germans.

It was now the early 1960s, but despite the moratorium on the pursuit and prosecution of Nazi sympathizers from the war, French Prime Minister Charles de Gaul personally saw to it that Deneque would be tried for his crimes. Because of his extreme treachery, the amnesty shown to other collaborators did not apply to him. Deneque was tried and found guilty in 1966 and sentenced to death. He mysteriously died in prison before the sentence was carried out, however. Apparently this often happened with convicted collaborators. They were viciously hated for their deeds even by the other prisoners.

Greg and I spoke and emailed several times since that day he reached out to tell me about Deneque, and from his research, he discovered that the French doctor that drove Jim and Don into Lille did not betray them. Dr. Leon Baron and his wife were dedicated members of the French underground, but apparently Marcel Deneque had known of the movement of the airmen from Belgium to France, and had informed the Germans of the route and the time of transfer. Deneque's cover was so tight that the Germans didn't even want the two Allied airmen to know what had happened, and by letting the French couple go after removing Jim and Don from the car, it made them believe that it was Dr. Baron and his wife who were the betrayers. What the two American aviators didn't know was that less than a kilometer down the road was another road block, and there the doctor and his wife were arrested by the Gestapo. Both ended up in concentration camps, the wife reportedly dying there. Dr. Baron died shortly after the war.

Until their dying day, Jim and Don, as well as most of the surviving Fowler crew, believed that this was why the two men ended up being captured instead of evading and being liberated as the others were.

Just when it seemed that it couldn't be more bizarre, another strange event took place.

Don had told me about an incident that occurred shortly after he had moved to Cape Girardeau to take the new job with the Missouri Department of Education. Out of the blue, he was visited by an agent of the United States Air Force Office of Special Investigations. He didn't remember the exact date, but it was shortly after he and his family had moved in order for him to take the new job, so it was in the early to mid-60's. Don told me that the investigator had asked him about his experience in Belgium after being shot down.

In particular, the investigator wanted to know the various places that he had hidden and who the Belgian citizens were that he had stayed with. He told me also that the investigating officer wanted to know if he had been to Belgium or France since the war. At that time he hadn't been back, and indicated as such.

I don't know if it was an assumption on his part, but he said that he felt that the investigator was following up on the death of the doctor who had delivered him to the Germans at the roadblock, and perhaps he was trying to find out if the doctor had been killed by one of the betrayed airmen.

Here's the twist to the story: Greg Celerse spoke to me in November 2019 and told me that he had obtained the report of the Air Force investigator, a Lt. Col. James W. Lovenbury. The report shows most of what Don had related to me with a couple of exceptions. Don didn't mention anything about a doctor and his wife taking him and Jim Fowler to Lille. He stated that they had traveled by bicycle and foot on the way to Lille until captured by the Germans. Colonel Lovenbury stated in the report that he had asked Don if the names Dr. Leon Baron or Marcel Deneque were familiar to him. Don told him that he did not know those people.

The discrepancies can be explained. I'm sure Don did not know Marcel Deneque, even though Deneque might have known him through observation or information gleaned from contacts in the Solre Saint Gery area. It was known that Amboise Baudart was working with the Nazis, and he was a local citizen. He was giving his information to another source, either directly or through secondary contacts.

In fact, it is very probable that Deneque could be the mysterious visitor to the Solre Saint Gery area that Sylvie Derenne told me about during my visit with her. According to Greg, Deneque worked the area of northern France and Southwestern Belgium, and there were various reports of unknown tradesmen visiting the Solre Saint Gery area.

As for Don telling the investigator that the name of Dr. Leon Baron was not familiar to him, it was probably because the Barons did not give Don or Jim their names. If they used names at all, they were probably using pseudonyms to protect their identity. This was a common practice with members of the underground, especially those with momentary contact with evadees.

In the matter of Don saying that he and Jim had traveled by foot and bicycle to Lille, I think that was a mistake on the part of the investigator. I remember Don telling me that they had traveled by foot and bicycle while moving from Belgium across the border into France to where they had connected with the doctor. That was also the story that Jim Fowler had told an interviewer in France.

Don and Jim were definitely taken to Lille by automobile but by people they did not know. There was no doubt that Don and Jim knew the people who took them into Lille as a "doctor and his wife", even though he may not have known their real names. He often told me about the doctor betraying them. There was even a remark made in the Missing Air Crew Report about he and Fowler being captured in France.

I recently was supplied with a copy of Jim Fowler's similar interview by Air Force intelligence, and it supported what Don had told them. He wasn't familiar with many of the people who had aided them, but was sure that they had been betrayed by someone who was familiar with their movements. Don never told me anything about any communication between him and Jim Fowler about this matter. I strongly feel that the incident of being betrayed by the doctor (even though it turned out not to be true) was a very bitter and painful memory for Don, and he simply wanted to put it behind him. I think that he felt that the investigator was looking into the death of the doctor, pursuing the slim possibility that Don or Jim had gone back to France to avenge their capture. Don had not gone to France, and knew that probably Jim hadn't either, so he wasn't too interested in helping the investigator. The true purpose of the investigation was to gather information for the prosecution of Marcel Deneque.

According to Greg, Deneque was so notorious in his crimes that he was being hit by everything that they could discover about his dealings with the Germans, and the United States Air Force had sent the investigator to try to gather any information that Don and/or Jim might have that could help the French in their prosecution. The report was submitted to the French government in 1965, just before Deneque went on trial.

Hardly anyone would have blamed Don or Jim for avenging their betrayal, but they didn't go to France to kill Dr. Baron, and the Air Force nor the French thought that they had. Perhaps the investigator should have disclosed the purpose of the interview, but the report that Greg sent me was marked "CONFIDENTIAL", so Lt. Col. Lovenbury might not have had the latitude to enable him to explain his intentions.

Finding out in 1965 that Dr. Leon Baron and his wife were not the betrayers that they had seemed to be might have eased Don's mind about how he and Jim had been captured.

Trying to piece together the last few weeks that Don and Jim spent in Belgium and their trip to Lille that resulted in their capture is a good example of how sometimes things just fall into place. If it hadn't been for the good fortune of "meeting" Greg Celerse over the internet, the solution wouldn't have come about. My wife Donna was intrigued by how I knew this information was correct. The short answer is that I don't know for sure, but we do know that Marcel Deneque did what he did, and the French investigators knew that he was operating in both Belgium and France. The bottom line is that we know that Deneque was active in betraying hundreds of French and Belgian underground members as well as scores of evading airmen. That is the crime for which he was found guilty. We also know that he was responsible for the capture of Dr. Leon Baron and his wife. We do not know for sure that he was responsible for the capture of Don and Jim, but it is likely that he was because of the close proximity of the capture of the two Americans and the Barons. Was he responsible for the capture of Sylvie and the others in Belgium? That we don't know, and I hope that new information might become available about that in the future.

He was important enough for the French to enlist the aid of an investigator with the Air Force Office of Special Investigations to interview Don, and to hopefully find knowledge that would bolster the prosecution against this traitor.

German records showed the capture of Dr. Baron and his wife, so we know that they were not the betrayers of Don and Jim as was first thought. Learning how Don and Jim traveled across the border from Belgium to France was always a missing piece of the puzzle, but I came across a recollection by Jim that was printed in a booklet about the underground and that was written in French. Getting it translated wasn't a problem, and it proved to be valuable in learning how the two airmen were handed off to several different "handlers" in both Belgium and France. The different people that worked with moving them were very secretive, and their very lives depended on not getting caught. But that same network invited problems for the same reason. It was difficult to know whom to trust. Deneque and his cohorts slipped in at some point, creating a crack in the network. Because of the fact that not any one person knew a great deal about the system, a few people were caught by the Germans, but not as many as it could have been.

Sylvie and her husband, perhaps her apprentice, Dr. Baron and his wife, Albert Rolin, and a few others were picked up, but it was a miracle that Dr. Verstraeten, a man who truly *did* know almost everything that was going on in the local underground, didn't get apprehended. And although things didn't work out for Don and Jim, none of the other members of the Fowler crew were ever discovered while being hidden. Like the men who fought in WWII, most of the members of the underground are now deceased, but through the efforts of people like Greg Celerse, maybe more of the secrets of underground will be revealed in the future.

Playing the devil's advocate, Donna asked me why Don and Jim weren't told by anyone at the dedication of the monument in Belgium in 1987 that the doctor and his wife were innocent of betraying them, and that Marcel Deneque was probably responsible. In all probability, nobody in Solre Saint Gery knew that. First of all, even though Lille isn't all that far from Solre Saint Gery, they are in two different countries. Secondly, even though there was interest in the history of the underground activity during WWII at that time, seeking and finding information was more difficult before the internet. Because of the availability of information and the easy access to old records through the internet, I was able to find the two German pilots that shot down the *G.I. Sheets*, but before that, all anyone knew was that it was shot down by two Focke Wulfs. That's the best example that I know of to show the availability of information now as compared to 1987.

I'm hoping I can find an English translation of Marcel Deneque's trial, because perhaps there is pro-of there about his movements into the area where the Fowler crew went down. According to Greg, who has seen the pertinent documents, he was the man who set up Dr. Leon Baron. I can't wait for Greg's book to be published!

In conclusion, I'd like to say that this has been a thoroughly interesting endeavor. It started by Donna saying that she thought it would be a good idea for me to write down some of the things that her dad had done during the war. It would be good for the grandchildren and great-grandchildren to know about their grandfather. What started out to be a few pages has morphed into a book, and what a story it tells! It's about ten American boys who left the farms and factories and grocery stores and schools to do their part to stop the Nazis from trying to conquer the world. The aim of Hitler's Reich was to ruthlessly kill everyone that didn't believe in their twisted cause, and it took the Americans to turn the tide in the war and put an end to it.

The war that they fought was the largest, longest, and most expensive and extensive that has ever been waged. Their experience in flying that last mission was a mixture of fear, bravery, and mistakes. The death of Miller Jackson was one too many, but it could have been much worse. Nine survived the war, but they never outlived it. It was always present in their minds, memories, and nightmares.

I'd like to give the reader a suggested book and movie to see that are the best that I've found for accuracy about what the bomber offensive prior to D-Day was like. The book is *Twelve O'Clock High,* by Beirne Lay, Jr., and Sy Bartlett. Both of the authors were part of the Eighth Air Force in England during the bomber war, and they wrote the book shortly after the war ended. The movie *Twelve O'Clock High*, adapted from the book, made its debut in 1949. Both the book and the movie are historically accurate without a lot of fluff. If the Blue Ray version of the DVD can be obtained, there are many bonus features about the war and how the film makers were striving for accuracy in the movie without a lot of Hollywood hype.

I've always been a fan of the old war movies, and as a kid I always thought that the real battles were fought by older men because that's what was portrayed by Hollywood. I came to realize that in the movies the characters were often played by older actors, but in reality, real wars were and still are fought by kids.

The average age of a bomber crewman in WWII was twenty-two-years-old. The average age of the Fowler crew was twenty-five. They were old men compared to most. As it was, Don was the youngest at twenty. He was old enough to go into battle, but not old enough to legally drink alcohol or vote. He was shot down and hiding from the Germans on his twenty-first birthday on March 30, 1944. It was a time and situation that few of our youth of similar age today can identify with. The boys who defeated the Germans and Japanese were truly "the greatest generation", to borrow a term from Tom Brokaw's book of the same title. All of us who came along after that war owe a debt to men like Don, a debt that we can never repay. The one thing that we *can* do is to try to learn and understand as much as possible about how WWII came about, and why thousands of young men in this country quit their jobs, left their farms and factories and schools, and went off to do whatever was necessary to defeat the enemy.

Grandpa often said that he survived the crash of the *G.I. Sheets* "on a wing and a prayer". We survived WWII because of lots of wings and lots of prayers, and lots of common men like Grandpa who fought with unselfish courage. *We must never forget them.*

Our lives are much richer for what was done by Grandpa Dinwiddie and the others of his generation. WWII was definitely our grandpas' war, and we owe it to them to never forget what they did. Telling this story about Grandpa Don Dinwiddie is my way of a pitifully inadequate "thank you" to him and his fellow airmen for their courage and dedication in the war that they successfully waged against the tyranny of the Nazis.

I'm sure there's a special place in Heaven for the men of the 303rd Bomb Group and the crew of the *G.I. Sheets*, and I hope that Miller Jackson was standing there beside St. Peter to welcome each of his fellow crewmen home from their last mission. And I hope that somewhere in this gathering was the wayward tail gunner, Harry Wallrobenstein, who found the courage to get back in the air, eventually flying more missions than any of them...

Terry Irwin
Gordonville, Missouri
June 21, 2020

CHRONOLOGY OF NOTABLE EVENTS

March 30, 1923

- Donald Jones Dinwiddie born to Archie and Irma Dinwiddie in Higbee, Missouri.

November 6, 1942

- Quits job in Remington plant, enlists in U.S. Army Air Force at Ft. Leavenworth, Kansas.

November 1942 to October 1943

- Basic Military Training, Wichita Falls, Texas
- Radio School, Truax Field, Wisconsin
- Gunnery School, Wendover Field, Utah
- Basic B-17 Crew Training, Pyote Field, Texas
- Advanced B-17 Crew Training, Dyersburg Field, Tennessee

November 3, 1943

- Arrived RAF Molesworth, Cambridge, England
- Assigned to 8th Air Force
- 41st Combat Wing
- 303rd Bomb Group
- 427th Squadron

December 11, 1943

- First bombing mission, Emden, Germany

December 13, 1943

- Second bombing mission, Bremen, Germany

December 24, 1943

- Third bombing mission, Vacqueriette, France

December 30, 1943

- Fourth bombing mission, Ludwigshafen, Germany

January 4, 1944

- Fifth bombing mission, Kiel, Germany

January 21, 1944

- Sixth bombing mission, Beaulieu, France

January 29, 1944

- Seventh bombing mission, Frankfurt, Germany
- Lost supercharger, Engine #2 while crossing Channel
- Lost Engine #4, eleven minutes from target, left formation
- Flak damage to aircraft, all crew except pilots wounded
- Attacked by four Me-109s, Thompson and Taylor badly wounded
- Attacked by two Focke Wulfs near Florennes, Belgium
- Jackson and Ferguson seriously wounded.
- Engine #3 destroyed, rudder controls inoperative, forced landing in farm field near Solre Saint Gery, Belgium
- Jackson dead, Taylor and Ferguson taken to hospital, Thompson taken by doctor
- All other crew members split up, all go into hiding

January 30, 1944

- Fowler crew officially listed as Missing In Action (MIA). Missing Air Crew Report file officially opened

March 1944

- Don and Jim Fowler meet with Arrington, Thompson and Zimmer for short visit

April 13, 1944

- German Gestapo raid Dr. Verstraeten home, no arrests

April 13, 1944

- Sylvie & Carme's home raided by Gestapo, both arrested

May 13, 1944

- Don and Jim captured by Germans in Lille, France

May 14, 1944

- Don taken to transfer and interrogation center Dulag Luft, meets Buddy Shaw from Fayette, MO

May 16, 1944

- Don arrives at POW camp Stalag Luft IV in Poland

May 23, 1944

- Copilot Barney Rawlings returns to England, reports that all crew were alive after crash except for Jackson

June 6, 1944

- Allied invasion at Normandy, Germans are soon retreating across France and Belgium

September 1944

- Arrington, Thompson, and Zimmer liberated by U.S. Army troops in Belgium

February 6, 1945

- Don and Stalag Luft IV POWs begin long forced march, walked 86 days, 600 miles

May 2, 1945

- Day 86 of forced march
- Don liberated by British 8th Army Royal Dragoons near Gudow, Germany

May 7, 1945

- Germany officially surrenders, war in Europe over.

May 15, 1945

- Don officially returned to U.S. Army control

October 28, 1945

- Don discharged from Army

June 24, 1949

- Body of Miller Jackson moved from Liege, Belgium and interred at Arlington National Cemetery, Virginia

October 1961

- Don, Jean, Donna and Kim move to Cape Girardeau, Missouri

Circa 1965

- Don interviewed by Lt. Colonel James W. Lovenbury regarding experiences in Belgium

June 5, 1986

- 303rd Bomb Group reunion in Fort Worth, Texas. Don, Fowler, Rawlings, Taylor, and Zimmer reunited for the first time in forty-two years.

June 27, 1987

- Dedication of the monument to the Fowler crew in Solre Saint Gery, Belgium. Don, Jim Fowler, Barney Rawlings, Loren Zimmer and their wives as well as the widow and son of Curtis Finley attended

February 19, 2005

- Don passes away, interment at Cape County Memorial Park, Cape Girardeau, Missouri

AFTERWORD

The Secret Army

For all practical purposes, the Fowler crew members were living on borrowed time. Most of them had flown at least eight missions without any real difficulty. Although the airplanes that had been assigned had taken hits, nothing put them out of action and nobody on the crew had been wounded. That is not to say that fear hadn't been present, because it was *always* there, and in abundant quantities. They had seen friends shot out of the sky, sometimes dramatically, as a direct hit by flak obliterated an aircraft in a blinding flash. They had seen fellow members of the 303rd carried out of returning aircraft dead or maimed from enemy flak or cannon shells. The fear and the reminders of war were always present, even though they seemed blessed with good fortune. Though they didn't talk about it, each of them had the dark thought in the back of his mind that something bad was bound to happen before the magical twenty-fifth mission would be completed. Even though they had the thought that lady luck would desert them sooner or later, they didn't expect her to turn on them so viciously as she did on that mission to Frankfurt on January 29, 1944. First the super charger went bad, then the flak damage to number three, having to leave formation, the attack by the Messerschmidts that severely wounded Taylor and Thompson, losing a prop, then breaking out of the clouds over the Luftwaffe field and being forced down by the Focke Wulf fighters and the ensuing wounding of Jack Ferguson and the death of Miller Jackson. Not only had Lady Luck forsaken them, she'd been taunting them for the entire mission.

One major serving of good fortune was that they had literally dropped out of the sky into the arms of some very dedicated Belgian resistance members, due only to the laws of physics and the benevolence of Oberleutnants Wolfgang Neu and Kurt Kranefeld. Even though the Fowler crew had trained and prepared for all sorts of emergencies that could put them on the ground, if the German pilots had desired, they could have blown them out of the sky that morning instead of allowing them to make the forced landing in the muddy field. Whether or not this was due to a German plan to let the men of that particular B-17 escape to be used as bait in an attempt to lure the resistance members into a trap, or if it was simply that Neu and his wingman saw no reason to blow an already-doomed aircraft out of the sky will never be known.

What is known is that as soon as the bomber slid to a stop in Marly's Field, the members of the Belgian underground were in charge of it. The fate of the crew was certainly in their hands at that point.

I, like many people, only knew about the European underground resistance because of what I'd seen in old war movies, or a paragraph here or there in a book. What I came to believe from that sparse information is that they were a ragtag bunch of poorly-equipped, ill-trained and vastly outnumbered civilians who were trying to fight a losing battle against the Nazi juggernaut. I never really had a great interest in learning more about the resistance members until I started to gather information on the story of the Fowler crew. I was surprised to find out that when I started my research, there wasn't a great deal of information available, but in the last few years, much previously classified material has been revealed. Much of this has come from revelations about how the Allies, particularly the United States and Great Britain, had worked closely to support partisan resistance cells in occupied Europe. Besides officially-released information, it is fortunate that many of the of the participants have also saw fit to write of their experiences and give us first person accounts of such an important part of the war.

In studying the new information available about the resistance movements, it was very evident that the Dutch, Belgian, and French underground organizations may have appeared "ragtag", and they were certainly outnumbered by the German military, but they were not disorganized nor ineffective in their mission. On the contrary, they were very organized, and because of their small numbers and their knowledge of their native geography, they were able to successfully pull off missions and obtain objectives that the larger (and for the most part, absent) Allied forces could not do.

It's been mentioned several times in this book that prior to the Allied invasion at Normandy on June 6, 1944 there were no British or U.S. troops in continental Europe. This is basically true, because there were no large forces in opposition to the Germans other than the air forces, but there *were* Allied personnel on the ground from the early days of the war. These people were known by many terms—spies, hidden assets, clandestine operatives—but by any name, they were British and American men and women who were put into place to work closely with the members of the Dutch, Belgian, and French underground. Before the buildup toward the D-Day invasion, the same policy (using some of the same operatives, in fact) was followed in the earlier campaign in the invasion and liberation of Italy. In actuality, planning for this type of operation began before the war had started.

Winston Churchill, born in 1875, was destined to become the Prime Minister of the United Kingdom in 1940, and served until the end of World War Two. He had another term as Prime Minister in the 1950s.

Churchill was known for being outspoken and for his love of the United Kingdom. Events of his early adult life shaped his handling of the British Isles during the second world war.

Churchill had a penchant for writing during his teenage years. When he was eighteen in 1893, he joined the British army and became a war correspondent in South Africa during the Boer War. In November of 1899 a train on which he was riding with British troops was stopped and captured by Boer forces, and he was taken prisoner and was placed in a prisoner of war camp. He soon managed to escape and was able to travel 300 miles back to British lines. During his evasion, he sought help from various friendly residents, without whose help would have resulted in his failing to succeed. He never forgot his experience. Later Churchill served in WWI and was successful as an infantry and cavalry officer. Although he was not taken prisoner during that war, many

British soldiers were, and again he saw that being able to use friendly French and Belgian residents allowed some to escape and evade capture by the Germans.

After WWI Churchill chose a career in politics, and by 1924 had achieved a position as a cabinet minister (Chancellor of the Exchequer). He was very outspoken on his feelings that Germany should not be allowed to rearm after being defeated in 1918. Later, during the rise of Adolph Hitler, he was very vocal in his warnings that dire problems would arise if he wasn't stopped. His feelings on both of these areas basically fell on deaf ears, and Germany *did* build a new military, and Hitler *did* come to power. Churchill became the Prime Minister in 1940, and successfully guided Britain through the war until 1945.

Even before being elected to the position of Prime Minister, and even before Hitler's forced invaded Poland on September 1, 1939, Churchill felt that Britain would be involved in the coming conflict, either by being invaded, or fighting to prevent an invasion. He remembered vividly his plight as a POW in the Boer War, and he knew that any war with Germany, whether on the continent or in the British Isles, would bring the need to aid men taken prisoner or trying to evade capture. He quietly urged those in the British intelligence office to begin planning for such a possibility. Because of his foresight, the Allies had an early advantage that allowed them to reap many benefits in addition to helping POWs.

While there is some overlap and always-present smoke and mirrors involved in any intelligence agency, during the research for this chapter I found no less than twenty-six different British intelligence offices being used in Great Britain from 1879 to the early 1950s. It was very clear in even a quick look at most of these that each agency was very protective of revealing its purpose and its secrets to sister agencies within its own country. During WWII there was more information shared, but the process was often carried out with reluctance. The particular British intelligence agencies discussed in this chapter are Special Operations Executive (SOE) and MI9 (British Directorate of Military Intelligence, Section 9). There was more than a little competition between these agencies and the "main" branch of British Intelligence, MI6. MI6 could be thought of as the wartime equivalent of the modern CIA of the United States. MI6 seemed to live in a constant state of fear that some of their power or, more importantly, their budget, would be usurped by the smaller units.

The primary duty of SOE was to carry out espionage, sabotage, and reconnaissance in German-occupied areas of Europe. This was carried out under the loose supervision of MI6, but since the purposes of SOE were these roles and none other, it could focus solely on getting the job done without much direct involvement of the parent group. SOE didn't like to divulge what they were doing for fear of having their operations compromised, so the activities it performed between 1939 and 1946 were for the most part top secret and not divulged until after the war.

MI9 was also a highly secretive part of British Intelligence that had two objectives: 1) aiding in the escape of Allied prisoners of war held by the Axis powers, especially those in German-occupied Europe, and 2) helping military personnel, especially downed aviators, trapped behind Axis lines, again particularly in German-occupied Europe. One of the major accomplishments of MI9 was in the development, aiding and supplying the escape lines and the partisans who operated them. Allied airmen were given rudimentary training on how the lines worked, cautions which they should exercise, and how to cooperate with the members of the underground. Especially for the Americans, who were new to European life and customs, this was an area of their early new-in-country orientation where few dozed off. The most interesting part of this training was that a large part of it was actually presented by downed airmen who had successfully evaded capture and had made it back to England. Like others before them, the Fowler crew listened to the lectures, but hoped they would not have to use the knowledge.

There were two "offices" of MI9 that worked intensely with escape and evasion and were operated with utmost secrecy. One was IS9(d), or "Intelligence School 9, Section D, sometimes referred to as "Room 900". This section was operated by James Langley and Airey Neave, both of whom had successfully evaded capture in German territory and had returned to England. Langley joined Room 900 in 1941, Neave in 1942.

These two men monitored returning evadees, debriefing all that returned to England in an attempt to learn the strengths and weaknesses in the operations of the various escape lines in order to maintain both secrecy and efficiency. It is interesting to note that upon his liberation in Belgium in September of 1944, Joseph Thompson of the Fowler crew was interrogated by Airey Neave. Thompson's report of this interview in his U.S. Army Air Force Missing Air Crew Report (MACR) upon his return to England was that he was upset that Neave didn't take seriously his observations of German troops that he had seen while hiding from the enemy. Not to denigrate Thompson's complaint, but at the time of his liberation, the Germans had been pushed eastward so far that there was little relevancy of what he had seen several months before.

The other office of MI9 was simply known as "Q". Q was operated by Christopher Hutton and Charles Fraser-Smith. The purpose of Q was to develop aids that could be used by escaped POWs and downed airmen. Things such as a small magnetic compass hidden in a tunic button, or a hollow boot heel that held dried food. They developed boots that were made with tops that could be removed to then create shoes that looked like that which would be worn by civilians. Q developed a successful method of smuggling information and maps into POW camps in parcels that were purportedly from charitable organizations, but in actuality were fake. Only after the Germans began to X-ray incoming parcels did the flow of secret maps, money, and even electronic components to build radio receivers, come to an end. If not for the imminent end of the war, Q would have probably overcome the X-ray problem, also.

If the office named "Q" sounds familiar, the reader is probably a fan of the James Bond books or movies. The Q of the novels was also the developer of all kinds of devices and contraptions that were given to 007 to help carry out his missions. This was no coincidence…Ian Fleming, the creator of the 007 character in the books and movies, was a veteran member of British Intelligence during WWII. Fleming wasn't working in an office, however, but was often involved in clandestine missions and commando raids.

As a side note, Fleming also wrote a children's novel called *Chitty-Chitty-Bang-Bang, the Talking Car,* which was a far cry from the spy business but became the basis for a successful movie in its own right.

Prior to the beginning of WWII, the intelligence offices of the United States were all tied to and dedicated to the various military services, plus one each that served the State Department and Treasury Department. President Roosevelt was fearful that the current system was failing to keep abreast of events unfolding in Europe and Asia. Urged on by officials in the British Intelligence office, Roosevelt appointed Colonel William J. Donovan to study the British MI6 and SOE units and develop a plan for a similar department to handle intelligence matters in the United States. In July of 1941, Donovan was appointed to the post of director of the newly established office of Coordinator of Information.

During the early days of Donovan's post, most of the intelligence information came from sources in the British intelligence units. Sadly, until after the Japanese attack on America's ships at Pearl Harbor, the military services did not treat the new Coordinator of Information as a viable resource, and in fact, treated its very existence with hostility. On June 13, 1942, Roosevelt issued a Presidential order creating a department called the Office of Strategic Services, with Donovan as the head. The duty of this new office was vaguely described as being in charge of "collecting and analyzing strategic information required by the Joint Chiefs of Staff and to conduct special operations not assigned to other agencies". In spite of the fact that the other military intelligence units as well as the FBI still did their own work as before the creation of the OSS, the powers given to the new office gave it great latitude. Colonel Donovan recruited personnel that engaged in a great deal of creative thinking in coming up with ideas about how to best carry out operations "not assigned to other agencies".

Some of the operations that were carried out were mundane, such as interviewing military personnel after being involved in battles or air missions. The interviews often reaped information about new kinds of defenses, vehicles (such as tanks), and weapons that the enemy was utilizing. Other operations weren't so sedate, such as the placement and communications with spies.

Once again, from old movies and spy novels, cloak and dagger operations are familiar to most of us, but this may be a case of truth being stranger than fiction. Many actual spy missions of British and American operatives were more dramatic and dangerous than anything fiction writers could dream up and put on paper.

One such example is the fact that several operatives used by SOE and OSS were actual Germans who had been captured and were POWs. Hitler and the Nazis were not popular with all German citizens or soldiers, and after an understandably thorough vetting by the intelligence agencies, some of former German military men were trusted with being dropped back into Germany or other occupied areas in order to observe and report back to the Allies. Most of these "turned" agents were not working on their own, but with other agents who constantly watched and controlled them. Most of them worked out, but some didn't. Such was the spy business.

To show how effective some agents were, two different Germans who were actually spying for the British were so good they were able to maintain contact and send data to England most of the war and continued to perform duties in the German army. The amazing part is that both of the agents were awarded the Iron Cross by Hitler for meritorious duty.

The American OSS was no less successful. Prior to the war, professional baseball player Morris Berg, who played for the Boston Red Sox, was on a special team that was playing exhibition ball in Japan. Berg, who had secret ties to military intelligence, pretended to be filming the games and tour related activities for MovietoneNews, a New York newsreel company. MovietoneNews provided him a camera and the necessary credentials. While Berg actually did film baseball activities, he also was able to sneak in film of the Tokyo harbor. He also was able to climb to the roof of one of the tallest buildings in Tokyo and film the city in all directions to locate possible strategic targets. Bear in mind this was done in 1934, during the time period that the Japanese were beginning to rattle their swords and were engaged in dominating the other countries in the Asian Pacific. While not vocal, there were members of the U.S. military that were trying to prepare for eventual conflicts with the Japanese, just as Churchill was preparing for the eventual war with Hitler.

Moe Berg, a Princeton-educated scholar, was not your typical baseball player, and was later recruited by the OSS as an agent during the war. He made several forays into areas in Europe to locate and gain information about the German atomic bomb and rocket projects.

Berg has the distinction of having the only baseball card on display in the headquarters of the present-day Central Intelligence Agency, the postwar version of the Office of Strategic Services.

While having agents on the ground was important to the activities of all of the intelligence services, the most important task was to maintain a connection with the native populations of the enemy-occupied countries.

Again, the very success of the eventual land invasion of Western Europe depended on getting the help of citizens that were living in the midst of the Germans. To underscore the importance of this, once again we have to compare the way war is waged in the 21st Century with the time of the 1940s.

Today, we can literally watch enemy troop movements in real time from satellites in space. If the need arises, we can dispatch an unmanned Predator drone from a Middle Eastern base to take out a particular vehicle several hundred miles away on a lonely desert road. The astounding thing is that the "pilot" flying the drone is in most cases sitting in a control room in Nevada or Arizona. He controls the drone from takeoff to retrieval, finds the target, fires the missile, and at the end of his duty shift, goes home to the suburbs. War fighters in WWII would think of this as science fiction.

During WWII, the most advanced technology was found in things like the Norden bombsight, German rocketry, and of course, the atomic bomb in the concluding days of the conflict. All of these things were touted as "secret weapons" at the time, and they certainly were. But there was no way to know enemy troop movements except for seeing it first hand. Fast recon aircraft could overfly enemy territory and take photos, but by the time those planes made it back to home base, the photos were developed (remember, no digital photos at that time), and analyzed, those enemy troops could be long on their way to another location. During the 1940s, the most valuable information was derived by human eyes on the enemy, and that information was then sent to those sources who could use it to fight the battles. The fastest means to get that information transmitted was by radio. Despite the fact that the internet didn't exist during WWII, radio signals still traveled at the same speed as today's email—186,000 miles per second. The problem is that radio is affected by atmospheric conditions, and the internet isn't. Using shortwave radio was reliable at certain times by trained operators, and it was the best thing available. It's fortunate that despite the drawbacks of radio, the distance from deep in Germany to England isn't that far for a radio signal to travel, and with the proper radio, antenna, and operator, sending messages over that distance is fairly easy. The problem was not to get caught while transmitting the messages.

Radios were the cutting edge in communications and media at the time of WWII, and radio communication took two forms in the intelligence world. First, mentioned above, was two-way communication in which an agent or underground member could transmit and receive messages. If one transmitted for too long a time period, however, the enemy had the capability of intercepting the transmission and by using a directional antenna, could get an approximation of the location of the transmitter. Naturally this was fraught with danger.

Another more benign method of transmitting information from Britain, or even the United States, was sending coded messaged via commercial broadcast stations. Through prior arrangement, certain code words or phrases broadcast from the British Broadcasting Corporation (BBC). For example, at a particular time on a particular day, could alert the underground members or an agent that supplies would be dropped at a certain time on a certain night at a prearranged location. This sounds sort of hit-and-miss as to accuracy, but it worked. By early 1944, certain phrases had been selected to inform the underground in France of the impending Allied invasion on D-Day. On the night before the invasion, it gave enough notice to certain operatives, who knew the code phrase, to perform certain activities in preparation for the invasion.

Another example of how commercial broadcast radio was used to give messages to underground groups was through giving a certain code word, then playing certain music. For example, the Polish underground was getting messages from the BBC through that manner. A particular fictitious announcer would be introduced (in this case it was usually "Peter Peterkin"), and Mr. Peterkin, speaking Polish, would give a brief introduction to a particular recording of a Polish musical composition that would then be played. The introduction and the particular music selection would be the code for the underground to perform a particular mission or expect further contact. Initially, problems were found with this method because programming engineers, who were not told of what was going on, would sometimes want to change the music. Later, intelligence operatives working at BBC made certain that once music was selected and approved, nobody could make changes. Theoretically, the wrong song being played could have resulted in the wrong bridge being blown up or the wrong person being assassinated. In spite of the obvious pitfalls, these commercial radio codes worked until there were better ways to perform two-way radio communication.

Besides the obvious problem with being able to communicate with agents and members of underground organizations, the most pressing issue that existed for the Allies was trying to solve the vexing situation of how to supply their personnel and the partisans on the continent, and the actual transportation of the people themselves. Methods of delivery of personnel, armament, money, and other supplies evolved as the war progressed. Many ideas were tried, and as primitive as some may seem, several actually worked.

Naturally, dropping supplies by boat could be done, since the English Channel is only a few miles across. The problem with that, obviously, is that German patrol boats could easily intercept such vessels, night or day.

This is not to say that fast boats didn't make some clandestine missions across the Channel, but it wasn't a dependable method. The obvious method, which could be used to go anywhere, theoretically, was by air.

The obvious problem, however, is that aircraft are large, noisy, and very noticeable, and they usually have to have large, flat surfaces on which to take off and land.

Only in the last few years have some of the previously classified details been released regarding the methods developed to deliver personnel and supplies into the enemy-occupied territories. One can see that necessity was definitely the mother of the invention of some of these techniques. It is also very apparent that the men and women involved in these clandestine activities were brave beyond measure.

As stated above, in the last few years there have been articles and books written about the topic of supplying and supporting the partisan groups in the German-occupied countries during WWII since that information has come to light. I will not attempt to retell this in detail, but for the reader to understand the workings of the Belgian and French underground organizations, and how this applied to the shelter and movement of the Fowler crew, I will give a thumbnail sketch of what a typical resupply mission would entail. The "typical" mission was usually anything but, and the pilots and crews of the aircraft involved never knew what surprises might meet them, but the missions that were planned were similar in nature and were carried out all over occupied Europe during most of the war, starting in earnest in late 1943 and increasing in number until the end of hostilities in May of 1945. There was a definite upsurge in missions just prior to and immediately after D-Day as partisan groups began equipping for and carrying out activities to support the invasion.

One of the missions flown by these clandestine aircraft and crews were radio intelligence flights. Using a particular radio known as "S phone", British Mosquitoes would fly low-level missions over a certain location where partisans were located with proper S phone equipment. Since the radio antennas were very directional, the short-range transmissions could only be heard if the aircraft and person on the ground were pointed in the right position. Using this technique, real-time communication could be carried out to get current information of German troop positions, etc. These flights were carried out under the auspices of the British IS9 WEA (Western Europe Area) office in conjunction with the United States Supreme Allied Expeditionary Force headquarters, commanded by General Dwight D. Eisenhower. The pilots who flew these missions wore a mysterious patch showing three witches on broomsticks. Such uniform patch displays were not usually allowed to be worn by crews flying clandestine missions, and the patches were only worn over a ten-month period. While the actual meaning of the three witches is not known, the common belief is that it was derived from the three witches found in the opening scene of Shakespeare's *MacBeth*. The symbolic message conveyed by the patch was that the three witches of the IS9 WEA were going to create "toil and trouble" for the enemy or to send the message "something wicked [from] this way comes", just as had been spoken by the witches in the play.

While radio intelligence missions were one of the secret missions flown by the British and American crews, the majority of the flights were "spies and supplies". Dropping agents into occupied countries along with the necessary supplies to outfit partisan groups were the missions of most crews. While these flights were commonplace from early 1944 to the end of the war, they were never routine. Every mission was secretive, and all were extremely dangerous.

Most of these missions were flown by American crews in modified B-24 bombers. The B-24 became their workhorse aircraft because it became available from a disbanded maritime submarine patrol group. The B-24 was fast and could carry a large load, but it was not an easy aircraft to fly low and slow. The preferred aircraft for this mission was the B-17, but unfortunately, they were in short supply and high demand for the Eighth Air Force's bombing campaign. At one point, General George C. Marshall, Chief of Staff of the Army, ordered that each bomb wing give up one B-17 for these clandestine flights, but before that could be carried out, the B-24s became available to fill the need. Some B-17s were used in the missions, as well as the Douglas A-26 and the aforementioned DeHavilland Mosquito.

In an earlier chapter of this book, I mentioned that three B-17s came off the assembly line at Douglas Aircraft in California in succession, all destined to go to the 303rd Bomb Group at Molesworth. All three made it there, but one of them, Production Number 42-39787, was taken out of service in January 1944 at the height of the bomber offensive. Coincidentally, this was the same time at which the order came down from the Chief of Staff for each bomb wing to give up one B-17 to the secret "spies and supplies" mission. The official records that I recovered on the history of this aircraft was that it did indeed end up back in the states and saw duty in Air Training Command in Texas and Florida prior to being scrapped at the end of the war in Arkansas. There was a gap in the records to give wonder that perhaps it was destined for spy duty but wasn't used after the B-24s were obtained. It was a big war with many airplanes and officers, and I'll always wonder if this one was "misplaced" after General Marshall's decree. For sure the timing was right for that to have happened.

What ultimately became the 492d Bomb Group, 856th, 857th, 858th and 859th Squadrons were tasked with flying the missions. They took the name "The Carpetbaggers" after the code name for their first mission. They were moved to a former British airfield, RAF Harrington, which was somewhat secluded and suited for the purpose of secretive flights. The B-24s were modified for their new role by removing the forward gun turret, the bottom ball turret, stripping out all unnecessary equipment to save weight, and getting a fresh coat of flat black paint. The hole in the fuselage where the bottom ball turret had been was used as an exit for agents to parachute from. The bomb racks were modified to carry specially designed, bomb-shaped cargo pods to carry the supplies dropped to the waiting members of the underground. The pods would be released in the same manner the bombs had been, but the cargo containers would have parachutes to slow their descent.

Missions would be normally flown on moonlit nights to allow better navigation at low levels. Most of the flights were flown at moderate altitudes in an attempt to stay below German search radar, and when reaching the drop site, altitudes were usually between 400 to 500 feet.

The usual crew would be a pilot, copilot, bombardier (who would drop the supply pods), radio operator, two gunners, and two navigators. One navigator would be in charge of the long distance navigation, and the other would be watching the landmarks on the ground to make sure of pinpointing the drop zone.

When the aircraft neared the agreed upon longitude and latitude of the drop zone, the navigators would watch for a particular arrangement of flashlights on the ground that would favorably compare with the planned drop direction. The pilot would circle, line up on the proper direction, and the agent would drop on a signal from the bombardier. The supply pods would also be jettisoned at the proper time. The entire process had to be performed accurately.

After the drop, the pilot would fly a course back to Harrington, and the cat-and-mouse game would have to be played with German night fighters. The return flight would usually be flown at low level in order to blend in with the ground and be more difficult to detect. With the advent of radar in later German night fighter aircraft, avoiding detection became more of a problem. One thing in the B-24s favor was that it was fast, and it did retain the top turret and the tail guns, and sharp-eyed gunners could often see German fighters sneaking in for the kill and ward them off.

After the D-Day invasion and as the Allied forces moved across France and Belgium, the Carpetbagger missions continued, but further into Europe, often into Germany itself. The Douglas A-26, a fast, twin-engine medium bomber, was found to be perfect for these deep missions. It could be over a target and gone before it was even noticed. Several agents were inserted into Berlin itself, and the drop zone for one agent was a city park near downtown.

When using the A-26, the word "drop" was certainly accurate. While it was a fast aircraft, it was not roomy. A plywood deck was built onto the actual bomb bay doors, and the agent or agents (it could carry two) had to lie on the plywood for the flight, with only a handhold to brace themselves on takeoff and while maneuvering. When they reached the drop point, they were given a brief warning, then the bomb doors would open and out they went. Needless to say, the A-26 wasn't the favorite ride of the agents, most of them wanting to have control of when they jumped.

The very low altitude in which the drops occurred was necessary to be able to hit the desired landing zone without the fear of wind drifting the pods and agents out of the area. The altitudes at which the drops were made were calculated to be the absolute lowest in which the chutes would open in time to slow the descent. Even at that, it was not uncommon for the agents to be banged up, and minor injuries were commonplace. The cargo pods, however, usually held up quite well. They had been designed in such a manner to survive hard impacts without damage or opening in the collision with the ground. The design varied with the objects that were being shipped. They were sturdy enough to protect explosives, and hand grenades and other high explosives were often delivered in this manner.

Bear in mind that the supplies that were dropped were being used by native partisans, most of whom were living double lives. By day they had their normal activities common to the average French, Dutch or Belgian citizen. By night, they may be a part of a sabotage mission, moving evading airmen along the escape line, or delivering secret information to other underground members. The supplies that were provided by the Allies were tailored to their needs. In today's high-tech era, the methods used in 1944 appear primitive, but they worked for the operation. One of the things that was often dropped were carrier pigeons.

The pigeons' home base was back in England, and once delivered to the underground, messages could be returned to the intelligence offices by bird. This proved to be a relatively fast and effective way for the area leader of an underground organization to send a "shopping list" of necessary supplies back to the delivery teams. The carrier pigeon system was quite acceptable for routine messages and didn't have the inherent risk of using shortwave and being tracked by the Germans.

Another seemingly odd shipment that was often dropped was money or other "valuable" cargo, such as jewelry. The money dropped was usually German, which was the common currency in the occupied areas. Jewelry and other valuable articles could be used by the partisans as objects of barter if using cash was too risky. The money was used mostly to allow the partisans to operate, and very often to keep the escape lines working. More often than not, the money was used for bribes, and to pay the expenses of making fake I.D.'s and other credentials. One Carpetbagger pilot remembered being told that one of his cargo pods contained over a half-million dollars in German currency, and that its delivery was high-priority. The purpose for such a large amount of money can only be imagined, but it surely wasn't a routine drop to fund a local partisan group.

Immediately before the Normandy Invasion on June 6, 1944, and for several months after, the OSS sent several teams of highly trained agents into France, Holland, and Belgium. The teams were usually teams of three, sometimes slightly larger, and their purpose was to infiltrate an area that needed observation or other preparation for a future Allied mission. The teams had a leader, a radio operator, and at least one member who fluently spoke the language of the area in which they were being inserted.

These groups operated under the code name "Jedburgh". The Jedburgh teams represented an early forerunner of what later became the basis for many of the special operation units that followed in the United States and Britain. The Green Berets, Navy Seals, and British Special Air Service (SAS) have honed the idea of the small, highly mobile and self-reliant unit that undertake difficult missions behind enemy lines. The Jedburgh teams were able to go into France prior to D-Day and work with native partisan units to assess German positions and locate possible targets worth of sabotage shortly before Allied troops arrived ashore. The teams were lightly equipped, carrying only the items necessary for their survival and the completion of the mission. Fighting knives and lightweight carbines and handguns were the only weapons they carried, and perhaps the most important item was the shortwave radio. Specially designed, small, and easily portable radios had been developed for their use, and they soon took on the nickname of the "Jed set". The Jed set enabled them to reach the necessary contact to relay recon information or to request aid. It also was a way to organize their extraction if necessary.

It is interesting to note that the teams were not always left "in country", so to speak. After the completion of some of the missions, the Jedburgh teams were often brought back to be trained and used again. As well as the Jeds, other personnel were also removed from hostile territory. This could be done the "hard" way by having them exit hostile territory via one of the escape lines, but that would be dangerous and time-consuming. Often, if the subjects needed immediate removal, there would be an aircraft sent to make a night landing in a large field in order to retrieve them. Usually the aircraft was something small enough to do the job, such as a single-engine British Lysander, but sometimes the larger twin-engine C-47 was used. Anything that could operate out of a large clear area was used. In today's special operations, there are aircraft that were designed with short, unimproved airfields in mind as part of their operating parameters from lessons learned in WWII.

It also must be kept in mind that not only the Jedburgh teams were dropped and retrieved. Of the many agents that were dropped into occupied Europe, many were also later extracted because of the value of their skills and training. Also, there were members of partisan groups that were extracted because of various reasons. Because of this, the Carpetbagger squadrons operated by carrying passengers and valuable cargo in both directions.

After the discussion in the chapter of how the underground members worked in cooperation with the mostly-absent Allied forces for most of the war, the question might arise as to how this involved the Fowler crew after their forced landing in Belgium. In fact, the interaction with the underground was there from the moment the bomber slid to a stop in Marly's Field.

If I had the opportunity to know what I know now, back in 1988 when I had the chance to speak to residents of Solre Saint Gery who helped the crew members, I'd ask about the organizational structure of their local partisan group. It is now evident that it *was* structured, and not a loose-knit group. When the bomber flew over, engines out, being chased to the ground by the two FW-190s, the wheels were put in motion by the members of the underground. Dr. Verstraeten was quickly notified, and it became very evident that he was, at least unofficially, the *de facto* leader of the local partisans. The fact that he was able to travel among the nearby communities definitely made him very useful, and I'm sure that the Germans certainly were watching him, and the fact that he was never caught was a testimony to his ingenuity and the secrecy of those he worked with and depended on.

It must be remembered that Rene Hannecart of Beaumont was considered the area "boss" of the underground and seemed to somehow get information from the Allies about the bigger picture of the war. He would coordinate what Verstraeten and the others would do. He was either in direct communication with a shortwave radio or was in communication with someone in the underground who was. If there were spies and supplies dropped to aid the local partisans, Hannecart probably new about it, but because of the compartmentalization of information, it was never conveyed to the others for fear of creating a serious leak.

Sylvie and Arthur Derenne, Maurice Lamendin, the Bouvigne family, farmer Albert Rolin, Father Paul Robert, Hermance Miot, Jean Dogne, and all who were actively helping to aid and hide the Fowler crew were all dedicated to fighting the occupying Germans even though there was great peril awaiting them if they slipped up. That certainly happened with the information that leaked to the Germans about Don and Jim's travel into France. Several people in the underground paid the price for that, ending up in German concentration camps, and Don and Jim being captured and sent to POW camps.

The entire operation of the underground depended on individuals who took chances. Everything revolved around keeping secrets and hoping to outfox the Germans. Even though there were failures and individuals paid the price, there was overall success.

Barney Rawlings made it down the escape line from Belgium to Spain, then back to England. Curt Finley almost made it, and if he had decided to stick with Rawlings, he would have probably made it back also.

The wounded on the crew were immediately taken to the hospital by Verstraeten and Lamendin, playing the part of the Good Samaritans that they were, but they did this under the noses of the Germans while they were hiding the other crewmembers. Don Dinwiddie and Jim Fowler were successfully hidden until they were betrayed by a Nazi sympathizer. Loren Zimmer, Joseph Thompson, and Richard Arrington were sheltered by the partisans until they were successfully liberated by the advancing Allied forces in September of '44.

Of the ten men on the crew, only one died in the line of duty. Four made it back to Molesworth unscathed. The two who were delivered to the hospital were immediately taken into custody by the Germans. Finley was being guided to freedom with Rawlings and probably wouldn't have been captured and made a POW if he had followed the escape plan put forth by the underground. Had they remained in hiding, perhaps Don and Jim would have been liberated in September along with Arrington, Thompson, and Zimmer. Had they not been betrayed by a French Nazi collaborator, maybe they would have made it back to England like Barney Rawlings. If Miller Jackson had kept wearing his flak vest, maybe he would have lived. Choices were made, and the fortunes of war were cast upon them.

The score of one dead, four successfully evading, and five surviving the war as POWs wasn't a bad ending when considering what could have occurred. All that happened was the result of the tenacity of the Fowler crew, the dedication of the members of the Belgian and French underground organizations, the foresight of Winston Churchill, the planning of the British and American intelligence services, and the daring of the agents who were delivered and supplied behind enemy lines by the pilots and crews of the Carpetbaggers.

ADDENDUM

The Myth of the Twenty-Five Mission Rule

A few weeks before this book was due to go to press, I stumbled across an important piece of information that totally transformed a belief that I had formed years ago, as far back as junior high. I found out that what I had always believed about the twenty-five-mission rule was not true. Thanks to my editor, Randy Baumgardner, I was allowed to put this last note in the book to explain. I'm sure I'm not the only person who has had the wrong idea about how many missions a bomber crewman had to complete and the process of being rotated out of combat.

As far back as I could remember, I had read in fact and fiction about the regulation that existed allowing a bomber crewman to fly twenty-five missions, and then be rotated back home as an instructor or being put in some other non-combat job. I had interviewed former bomber crew members who spoke of the quest for that twenty-fifth mission. It was even the central theme of the story of the *Memphis Belle*, for those who remember the movie or the wartime documentary. It seemed like every member of every crew was always counting the missions, waiting and dreaming of Mission number twenty-five.

A few days before writing this endnote, I came across a document produced by the USAF Historical Division entitled "Combat Crew Rotation, World War II and Korean War". This work details the problems and evolution of crew rotation from the beginning of World War II, through the Korean War, and actually into the Vietnam conflict, since it was written in 1968. It was an eye-opener, and I'm happy that we could fit it into my book since I mention the twenty-five-mission goal several times, and how most crewmen never made it to that point. Perhaps this addendum will help make sense of the whole idea.

Long before World War II and the most expansive air campaign ever waged, it was well-known that fighting men wear out, both physically and mentally, after constant combat. Shortly after the United States entered the war and started flying strategic bombing missions, it was evident that this new type of warfare had new twists on that old problem. Bombing missions were fraught with stressful situations: enemy fighters, anti-aircraft fire, and the tedious effort required in flying tight formations for several hours at a time. To make it worse, the role of the bomber was to hold its position at all times, and there were no aggressive maneuvers that could be performed to avoid enemy fighters or flak.

Unlike fighter pilots, bomber pilots had to basically fly a steady path, and hope their gunners could repel the enemy fighters. This was both physically and psychologically wearing on the flight crews. An added element of fear was the flak. With enemy fighter planes, the gunners could at least shoot back, but with flak, there was nothing to be done. As I mentioned earlier in this book, flak was insidious, coming at you from out of nowhere, unseen and deadly. Another problem for both mind and body was the high altitude and the bitter cold that came with it. Cases of frostbite and oxygen starvation were prevalent.

Aside from the actual things that could wound or kill you, the constant fear was worse. Surviving a mission and coming home was a relief, but it seemed that as soon as that mission was done, the fear of the next mission started to gnaw at most crew members. Most bomber personnel admitted that the fear of the unknown was worse than the fear present in actual combat.

None of this was lost on the commanders of the various bomber units, nor was it unnoticed by the commanding general of the Air Force, Hap Arnold. Everyone in the command structure, for the most part, knew that the stress and fear of this type of flying would wear down the individuals flying the missions. The problem was that nobody knew how much was too much. If the limits were identified, the other problem would be finding the replacements for the crew members being rotated out of combat flying. It was very apparent early in the war that flying the missions was very stressful and dangerous, and at the same time, that the process of training new replacement personnel back in the States would be unable to keep pace with a rotation schedule that was necessary.

As a starting point, in July 1942, the War Department established a one-year tour of duty for Army Air Force combat crews. In the early days of the bombing campaign, it quickly became apparent that this was unrealistic, and that plan was dropped without being put into operation. Instead, leeway was granted to the field commanders in the various theaters of operation to establish their own programs of how to address combat stressed flight crews. The general trend was toward plans that utilized the number of completed missions, flight hours, the types of missions, and the individual crew member's time in the combat theater of operation. Different commanders came up with different variations of the above criteria, and therein lay confusion. There was no simple "twenty-five-mission and go home" rule. To make matters worse, it was made quite clear to all personnel that even if they were rotated back to the States or another non-combat assignment, the needs of war would take precedent and they could expect to be brought back into the combat theater if necessary. For those few men who had actually made it to the point when they were taken out of combat, there was a requirement to sign documents to the effect that they were aware they weren't being permanently removed from the fighting, and would probably have to return to combat in the future.

More often than not, especially early in the war when replacements were hard to obtain, many crewmen came close to whatever the magic number was, but then found that the formula for rotation out of combat had changed, and they had to fly more missions. Needless to say, morale became a problem.

In an effort to ease the rotation problem while replacements were hard to obtain, there was a period when crews were taken out of duty temporarily and were allowed to go back to the States for a period of leave. This plan didn't work out well, because the visit back home was enough to make the return to combat more difficult and fearful. In an attempt to retain pilots in the combat theater, there was a plan implemented to allow pilots who had flown a certain number of missions and hours to transfer out of bombers into fighters or transports, but this proved a failure for the most part. Combat was the problem, not the type of aircraft flown.

The problem of what to do with the battle-worn flight crews remained from the beginning weeks of the war in 1942 until early 1944. There were no magic solutions proposed by any of the field commanders or other generals. The problem was fixed by two things: we were winning the war against the Germans, and the training of replacement flight crews back in the States was a huge success.

There are all sorts of related facts and stories that could be examined relating to the "twenty-five missions and home" myth, but in truth, despite what I and others have seen in books and movies, no solid rule like that ever existed. The variations on it that were proposed by different commanders really never worked, and the pressure was taken off of the flight crews by the training back home and the demise of the German Luftwaffe. The Allied air forces simply outfought the Germans and the Japanese, and we were training new pilots faster than they could.

Sadly, the good intentions of trying to find a workable way to rotate crews out of combat caused a great deal of mental anguish for the flight crews. They wanted to think that they would finally be told that they had done their part and be sent home, but nothing seemed to be real, just empty promises. It is no wonder that some men, like Harry Wallrobenstein on the Fowler crew, finally hit a breaking point. He went AWOL, but some openly defied orders and refused to fly. At any rate, many officers and non-coms chose to face disciplinary action rather than flying in combat. Others openly admitted that they couldn't fly (possibly navigator Joe Thompson), and were grounded for a time to rethink the matter. Most commanders felt that it was better for the rest of the crew not to have the liability of flying with an unpredictable member of the crew. Some, like Wallrobenstein, found their courage and went back to flying, but many didn't. Being told there was a light at the end of the tunnel, and then having the rules changed, caused added psychological pressure. Countering that, there were some crew members, like Woody Woddrup, who seemed to enjoy combat flying and flew every mission available. All of this needs to be tempered by the statistical fact that most bomber crews prior to mid-1944 never had much of a chance at making it past ten missions, much less twenty-five, so no wonder few crews went home after twenty-five missions. Few made it to that point, but everyone sought it.

There are two things worth noting in the USAF study of flight crew rotation policies in World War II and the Korean War. First, no workable solution was ever found during World War II (or the Korean conflict), but the problem was fixed by Air Training Command's efficient production of replacements and the successful fight against the Axis.

The second notable thing? Neither the Germans nor the Japanese had any plans or intentions of rotating their pilots and crews out of combat. They flew until they were killed or captured. By the closing months of the war, our enemies had resorted to the use of very young and poorly trained pilots, with disastrous results.

As mentioned earlier, the reader should find a copy of *Twelve O'Clock High* or watch the movie based on the book. The central theme, accurately developed and portrayed, was about exploring the limits of how far to push the bomber crews, and the disastrous results of going too far.

Terry H. Irwin and his 1946 Aeronca Champ.

ABOUT THE AUTHOR

Terry H. Irwin was born and raised in Southeast Missouri, a descendant of English immigrants that came to this part of the United States before the Civil War (on his maternal side) and in the 1880s (on his paternal side). They were instrumental in clearing the lowlands of Southeast Missouri and helping to create the fertile farmland that it is today. The flat farmland of the area was a perfect location of flight training airfields during World War II into the early 1960s. Irwin credits the T-28 trainers from Malden Air Base in Malden, Missouri and the crop dusters flying over the local farms as creating his lasting love of flying and aviation.

Irwin first started learning to fly at age 17 in the same 1946 Aeronca Champ that he presently owns and flies. He has earned his commercial pilot license and has been an active flight instructor since 1973.

He is a proud graduate of Oran High School, Class of 1969, and went on to earn his bachelor's and master's degrees in education from Southeast Missouri State University. He spent thirty-four years as an educator at the high school and college level.

Irwin and his wife, Donna (Dinwiddie), live in the Cape Girardeau, Missouri area. They have four children and seven grandchildren.

Sgt. Dinwiddie's War is his first book.

INDEX